THE WILL ROGERS BOOK

The Will Rogers Book

compiled by

PAULA McSPADDEN LOVE

Curator, WILL ROGERS MEMORIAL

Claremore, Oklahoma

 THE **BOBBS-MERRILL** COMPANY, INC.
A SUBSIDIARY OF HOWARD W. SAMS & CO., INC.
Publishers • INDIANAPOLIS • NEW YORK

Copyright © 1961 by Paula M. Love
Printed in the United States of America
First Edition
Library of Congress Catalog Card Number: 61-13153

To

Bill, Mary and Jim Rogers,
who I feel are also
"my children."

FOREWORD

Will Rogers was my mother's brother, and from my earliest childhood I loved my Uncle Will devotedly.

We lived in the small town of Chelsea, eighteen miles from Claremore, Oklahoma, in a home called "Maplewood." My mother was Will's "Sister Sallie." His other sister, our beloved Aunt Maud (Lane), lived across town at spacious "Sunset Farm." The two sisters were past masters in the art of entertaining, and my own sisters and cousins were trained to help in any kind of social activity. The two hospitable homes were always filled with company—usually kinfolk—but the biggest event in the lives of these sisters was their "Brother Will" coming home to visit.

My first recollection of Uncle Will is his ceaseless working with his ropes in our front yard, with a group of spectators around him. Sometimes he had us children ride by on our ponies so he could practice certain catches of both horse and rider. This game would go on for hours, and it was all business with him.

My happiest memories are of the period shortly after he had married the beautiful and captivating Betty Blake. We all adored her, for she seemed to have a special aura about her. I love to think back to the wonderful evenings when, after a bountiful dinner, we all filed into the parlor for a "program." Aunt Betty, a musician of exceptional ability, would take her place at the piano, and together she and Uncle Will would sing the musical hits of the day. Uncle Will would imitate other actors and their stunts, and tell stories and jokes like the master showman he was.

Often he would break into a buck-and-wing dance while Aunt Betty whistled the song to a banjo or piano accompaniment. Thus they brought Broadway and all its wonders to the well-filled room of relatives and friends. None of us then had the foresight to realize that Will would one day become so famous.

After the Rogerses had established their home in California, I spent a great deal of time with them and was very close to their entire family. Uncle Will and Aunt Betty did not love me any more than they did the other relatives, but because I had been lame since childhood, they tried to compensate for some of the things they felt I had been denied. They—bless them both!—turned my limitations into happy privileges that enabled me to enjoy life to the fullest extent.

When the state of Oklahoma built the impressive Will Rogers Memorial in Claremore in 1938, the Memorial Commission asked my husband, Robert W. Love, to take over the entire management of it. They named me curator. Here we have visited with many of the twelve hundred daily visitors who pass in and out of its doors. Almost without exception they have expressed a desire to read the things Will Rogers said.

It is from them and the requests that have flooded in by mail and telephone for certain Will Rogers "quotes" that the inspiration for this book came. My husband and I began to see the importance of preserving Will Rogers' writings and other related material, and began to build a research library. Rogers' fans contributed a great number of scrapbooks, clippings, letters, and other items. The University of Tulsa lent us their microfilm of the Tulsa *Daily World*, which enabled us to determine the correct dates for Will Rogers' articles and to arrange his works in chronological order. Homer Croy described this collection as being "packed with gold like a crib with yellow dent corn."

Bill and Jim Rogers approved of our making this collection and have given their consent to the use of their father's material.

In this volume I have not tried to write a book about Will Rogers. I have only compiled some of his priceless statements in an effort to preserve them.

PAULA McSPADDEN LOVE

CONTENTS

ILLUSTRATIONS

INTRODUCTION

Will Rogers, The Writer

Cowboy, trick roper, comedian, movie star, humorist, radio commentator, newspaper columnist, citizen of the world, philosopher, humanitarian, ambassador of Good Will, and many more appellations have been applied to Will Rogers, and he filled each one with distinction. But it was as a writer and a speaker that he became America's common-sense philosopher who will be remembered through the ages.

The people who were Will's contemporaries have an entirely different feeling for him from those of a later generation. Since he was able to project his inimitable personality into all kinds and classes of people, he became a part of every family. His insight into human foibles and events, his intolerance of injustice and chicanery, and his sympathy for the unfortunate and suffering were evidenced in the things he said as he played on the heart-strings of America, sensing the truth and tragedy of events and often turning the most tense situation into one of mirth.

All this was voiced by Herbert Hoover not too long ago when he said, "Our country has lost its sense of humor. We need an American humorist. There's been no one since Will Rogers."[1]

Because of his different ways of reaching people, Will Rogers was the most beloved man of his time. He died at the age of fifty-five at the height of his career— America's most popular public speaker; the biggest box-

[1] Nanette Kutner, "Herbert Hoover Today," *The American Weekly,* August 10, 1958.

office attraction in the movies; the most widely read of any of the newspaper feature writers.

His witty comments on persons and public issues, his humble, self-effacing manner, and his unfailing good humor were as familiar to the people as the air they breathed. He was not one person on the stage and another in public life. He was always Will Rogers, the spokesman and safety valve for America. He had learned early in his career that it was the way he talked and the things he said that brought the applause, so he remained natural and completely unspoiled as his fame and fortune soared.

"I am just an old country boy," he wrote. "I have been eating pretty regular and the reason I have is, I have stayed an old country boy."[2]

Will did not aspire to be a writer. It was his early ambition to be the best trick roper in America. He achieved that goal, but he also developed into a forceful and much sought-after speaker. He was perhaps more surprised than anyone else when he found out that people wanted to remember the things he said. They liked to discuss them and ponder the wisdom of his funny, often salty quips long after the laughter had subsided.

Will's first book, *The Cowboy's Philosophy on the Peace Conference*, was published in May 1919, and in August of the same year *The Cowboy's Philosophy on Prohibition* appeared. Both of these small books were collections of the jokes, or "gags" as he called them, that he used in his act in the *Ziegfeld Follies* and the *Midnight Frolic*.

His success as a speaker in the years that followed brought him to the attention of editors. They felt that any man who could hold an audience and entertain them as he did would be a very popular writer. V. V. McNitt of the McNaught Syndicate approached him at the *Follies*

2 Weekly article, August 31, 1924.

16

to see if he would write for them. As usual Will was reluctant to try anything in this medium. Up to this time he had written only brief and occasional humorous articles for various papers, and he had not yet reached his stride in writing. In the meantime the *New York Times* offered him $150 a week to write his comments on the daily news, which he readily accepted.

On December 31, 1922, he began his series of weekly articles which were released through the McNaught Syndicate. These appeared in the Sunday editions of the papers, expressing his views on current events in true Rogersesque manner. "Slipping the Lariat Over," the *New York Times* called the column; the Los Angeles *Examiner* selected "Roping the News" for its title. Other papers wrote their own headings, such as "Will Rogers Settles the Affairs of the U.S. Without Cost to the Taxpayer." In 1924 a collection of these articles on a diversity of subjects was published under the title *The Illiterate Digest*.

In September 1924 he was engaged by the American Tobacco Company—"to write for us 26 pieces of *Bull Durham* copy, each to be signed by you," the contract read, "and to be approximately 150 words in length and to permit the publication of an illustration of yourself as a part of each advertisement."[3] He began with the following, which was something unusual in the field of advertising:

I know you people are going to say "What do you think of Will Rogers writing and endorsing 'Bull Durham'?" That's where you're wrong. I am not endorsing it. I never smoked any tobacco in my life, not even Bull Durham.

3 Letter dated September 29, 1924, from Frank W. Harwood to Will Rogers.

If you want to know the real truth why I signed up to write a lot of pieces for these people it's because I love animals. Have you ever studied the picture of the Bull carefully? Have you ever seen such a kind looking animal? I thought this: Certainly no one who cares as much about dumb creatures as they do would put out anything but the best smoking tobacco possible. So I said, "All right, I'll write your stuff." Honestly, the money part of it dident have much to do with it. That is, not very much. . . .[4]

Each of the Bull Durham ads was on a different subject, and Will used many of them later for full-length weekly articles

He began writing "The Worst Story I've Heard Today" on May 15, 1925, and continued it until January 15, 1927. This was a daily article and was also released through the McNaught Syndicate. His first story was on the Prince of Wales,[5] who was visiting America at that time. As usual Will wrote about everybody from such leading political figures of the day as Al Smith, Governor Hylan of New York, Barney Baruch, and the mayors of different cities; actors of the theatrical and movie worlds; baseball players; Oscar, the chef of the old Waldorf. Of course, Oklahomans came in for a fair share of stories and even such obscure individuals as his sister's hired man. It was not so much the story he related that pleased his readers as it was the "build up" he gave the person who had told the story. These articles also gave an account of the places he went and some of the people he met, for he

[4] Bull Durham advertisement #1 (proof from H. W. Kastor & Sons Advertising, New York, Chicago, St. Louis), Scrap Book #7.
[5] The present Duke of Windsor.

had started his lecture tours in October of 1925. These articles were the beginning of what was later to develop into his famous daily telegram.

In the spring of 1926 he went to Europe to do a series of articles for *The Saturday Evening Post*. He called the series "Letters of a Self-Made Diplomat to His President." These were addressed to the then President of the United States, Calvin Coolidge, who, of course, was quite innocent of the matter. Some of the best of Rogers' humor is in this series of vivid accounts of his interviews with the leading figures of foreign countries and his visits to the tourist attractions and resorts. The "Letters" were so popular that they were brought out in book form that year under the same title.

While he was in London, he sent a collect cable to the *New York Times* which read:

> July 29, 1926: Nancy Astor, which is the Non de Plume of Lady Astor, is arriving on your side about now. She is the best friend America has here. Please ask my friend Jimmie Walker to have New York take good care of her. She is the only one over here that don't throw rocks at American tourists.
>
> Yours respectfully,
Will Rogers[6]

The late Joseph Tebeau, the night managing editor of the *Times*, ordered the piece published on the first page of the second section. With no further arrangement as to space or renumeration, Will continued to send the daily wires to the *Times* from wherever he was in Europe until he returned home in the fall.

6 First daily telegram, July 29, 1926.

The squib was tremendously popular, and the editors of the *New York Times* were delighted to have this exclusive. The McNaught people were well aware of its potentialities. McNitt was also in Europe that summer and made every effort to find Will and sign him up for the article. Whether or not he did so is unknown, but Will did have the following "Worst Story" on McNitt:

September 10, 1926. Worst Story

The Worst Joke I heard today was told me by V. V. McNitt. V. V. is the owner of the McNaught Syndicate of New York. Well, he is over here in London, he and his family, and has been prowling around all over Europe. He has been up to Scotland. I am not sure but I think Mac has a touch of Scotch, and you ever let one of the Scotchmen get over here and he just breaks out for the Heather again like a milk-pen calf to its mother when it gets out. Scotland is having pretty tough sledding now. The Irish since they got freedom are about to come over and take it way from the Scots. Mac had some Scotch yarns to relate. An American who had taken a shooting Lodge in Scotland, got lost one day in the heavy mist and was tramping around and couldn't find his way back. Finally he heard footsteps and looked around and there was a Scotch native of the Moors.

"I'm lost," said the American.

The old Scotch mountaineer answered him. "I know you are lost, but is there any reward for finding you?"[7]

[7] Tulsa *Daily World,* September 10, 1926 (microfilm).

20

October 14, 1926, Will began his daily telegram captioned "Will Rogers Says," by which he became so well known. This was handled by the McNaught people. It began with ninety-two papers subscribing to the article, a number that increased to over five hundred. The McNaught Syndicate was the only one that ever handled his newspaper articles. He was fond of the men on the staff and appreciated the way they had treated him when he was beginning to write. He always held a warm feeling for the *New York Times*, as shown in the following daily telegram:

April 9, 1935: My boss is dead. Adolph O. Ochs, owner of the great New York Times is the first man I ever wrote for and it was him personally that got me to try it. Think of being lucky enough to break in at the top, for that paper is tops.[8]

While he was in Europe, he flew to Russia—in August 1926—and as a result of that trip wrote *There's Not a Bathing Suit in Russia*, which was published in 1927. This is one of the best efforts in his field of writing.

After a strenuous lecture tour in 1927 he returned to his California home quite ill. Despite the physical pain and the inconvenience of being unable to do for himself, his thoughts turned to his daily telegram. Summoning Mrs. Rogers to his bedside, he dictated the following wire for release the next day:

June 16, 1927: Here is where the joke writers and everybody get even with me. I am in the California hospital where they are goint to relieve me of surplus gall, much to the politicians' delight.[9]

8 Daily telegram, Tulsa *Daily World* (microfilm).
9 Daily telegram, Tulsa *Daily World* (microfilm).

Though the operation was a serious one and he was gravely ill, he made good use of the experience later on by recounting it in rollicking detail for *The Saturday Evening Post* and also on the lecture platform. It was issued in book form under the title *Ether and Me,* and is still today a popular book. It was the last of the six books Will published.

He wrote other articles for *The Saturday Evening Post,* which he called "More Letters of a Self-Made Diplomat to His President." These were about his trips to Mexico, and "Letters" to the leading political figures of the day. He wrote articles for the *American Magazine* and introductions to the two Charles Russell books, *Trails Plowed Under* and *Good Medicine*; C. R. Coopers' *Annie Oakley, Woman at Arms*; Chester Byers' *Roping*; and *Around the World in Eight Days* by Wiley Post and Harold Gatty; and even an introduction to a cook book the ladies of Beverly Hills got out.

The old *Life* ran him for President in 1928 when Robert Sherwood was its editor. He wrote some short articles for this magazine, calling his the "Anti-Bunk Party." In them he analyzed the "Political Hooch."

"The greatest name in entertainment is coupled with the greatest name in rubber for your benefit" ran the advertising in the copy Will wrote for the Goodyear Rubber Company in 1929. This was a postal card campaign, and one of Will's ads went like this:

"The whole business of politics is based on "Expelling Air." Who would have ever thought a giant industry could be built up on "coralling" air. When air goes in a Goodyear tire, it's like going to Sing-Sing for life."[10]

10 #002, Rogers Collection, Will Rogers Memorial.

It did not seem difficult for Will to write, and he could write anything for anybody at any time. He could not answer all the requests that came to him, but he kept up his weekly articles and his daily telegrams to the end of his life.

Wherever he went, he carried a portable typewriter with him and pecked out his articles with his middle fingers at an amazing rate of speed. In the crashed airplane that took his life was found his typewriter with an unfinished weekly article still in the machine. The last word that he had written was "death."[11]

When Will made the transition from monologist to writer, he kept the same personality he had employed on the stage. He wrote as he talked, in an informal intimate manner with no regard for grammar, syntax, or the formal rules of English. He used capital letters at random and a generous supply of commas; occasionally a period would find its way in. He spelled words as they sounded to him, giving them a misshapen, foreign appearance, but this eccentricity only added to the humor of the pieces. He made excessive use of such words as *dident, hadent, aint, 'em* (for *them*), *cuckoo, baloney, hooey,* and *applesauce.*

He had asked the syndicate to print his articles as he wrote them with no editing, and it complied with his wishes. His was a style all his own, set down in his peculiar, homely, often careless but understandable manner. As he explained, "When I write 'em, I'm through with 'em. I'm not being paid reading wages. You can always see too many things you wish you hadent said, and not enought that you ought."[12]

We miss much of the typical Rogers' humor in only the printed word, for Will was primarily a speaker and a show-

11 Weekly article, Will Rogers Memorial (unpublished manuscript).
12 Weekly article, September 1, 1929.

man who knew to the split second the timing of a joke or when to bring in the applause line. Some of his statements are classics and timeless; others have to be supplied with background as he wrote on the then present-day situations. However, reading Will Rogers day by day, one gets a very comprehensive history of the United States during the years he wrote.

Will Rogers is one of the most quoted Americans. People love to hear again the things he said. His was an earthy and spontaneous humor that came straight from his own ingenuity and reached the hearts of the American people who were waiting for his interpretation of the events of the day.

THE WILL ROGERS BOOK

AMERICA, U.S.A.

The Country

1. There's no other country with as much air, and not knowing where it's going as this country.

2. A Country has got to be based on settlers, not grafters.

3. That's what's the matter with this country. It's been advised to death. An editorial might explain the right course for everyone to pursue, but who wants to pursue it.

4. You can *diplomat* America out of almost everything she has but dont try to bluff her.

5. We are always doing something through the kitchen

door. We like the glory but not the responsibility.

6. It will take America fifteen years steady taking care of our own business and letting everybody else's alone to get us back to where everybody speaks to us again.

7. [At Democratic meeting.] Aint it wonderful to have something come up in a country where you can find out just how many political cowards there are?

8. Now if there is one thing that we do worse than any other nation, it is try and manage somebody else's affairs.

9. America invents everything, but the trouble is we get tired of it the minute the new is wore off.

10. What this country needs is more working men and fewer politicians.

11. The world is with the fellow coming up. Let the fellow that's already up look after himself. Every crowd wants to see a new champion crowned.

12. If you can do anything better than anybody else this old country is so constituted they want to see you get all you can out of it.

13. The trouble with America is we cant even seem to see somebody else only through our eyes. We dont take into consideration their angle or viewpoint. You see, everyone of us in the world have an audience to play to; we study them and we try and do it so it will appeal to what we think is the great majority. So we all have our own particular little line of applesauce for each occasion. So let's be honest with ourselves and not take ourselves too serious, and never condemn the other fellow for doing what we are doing every day, only·in a different way.

14. [Luncheon clubs] have to be against something or they wouldent be formed. This old thing of eating at home with the folks is never going to get you any-where. No real AMERICANISM in that.

15. We got as much [rumors of foreign war] as we've ever had. There is just as much money, as many to eat and as many to feed, as many to buy, but our conditions are uncertain. Because this thing outside our own land is worrying 'em. The whole thing is world wide. We

are effected by it less than anyone. If we keep our nose clean and dont start yapping about somebody else's honor, or what our moral obligations are, we might escape it. But it's going to take better statesmanship than we have been favored with heretofore.

16. We might be the wealthiest nation that ever existed, we might dominate the world in lots of things and because we are richer than all our neighbors or than anybody else, that dont necessarily mean that we are happier or really better off. The difference between our rich and poor grows greater every year. Our distribution of wealth is getting more uneven all the time. We are always reading "How many men paid over a million dollar income tax" but we never read about "how many there are that are not eating regular."

17. But in all it's a great country. It's the best and the worst one I ever lived in, and I been living in countrys for 54 years next November fourth.

The People

18. We are a people that get tired of a thing awful quick and I believe this continual prosperity will begin to get monotonous with us. We cant go through life just eating cake all the time. Of course, we like prosperity but we are having so much of it that we just cant afford it.

30

19. The American people are generous and will forgive almost any weakness with the exception of stupidity.

20. [American people] like to have you repent; then they are generous.

21. Nobody wants to be called common people, especially common people.

22. They tell you we are living in a fast age. We are . . . if we can live.

23. We do more talking progress than we do progressing.

24. The public dont care how you go to college, it's how you are going to get from the forty yard line to over the goal that they are worrying about. We are a "get the dough" people and our children are born in a commercial age. Why if a babe in arms can cry loud enough to get paid for it we are tickled to death. Make 'em pay for talent whether it's art, music, football, literature, radio announcing or flag pole sitting. Any actors that can draw 88 thousand people in one day is worthy of their hire. Dont let Wall Street get all the gravy.

31

25. People's minds are changed through observation and not through argument.

26. There is still a lot of monkey in us. Throw anything you want into our cage and we will give it serious consideration.

27. The Romans loved blood. What money is to an American, blood was to a Roman. A Roman was never so happy as when he saw someone bleeding. That was his sense of humor, just like ours is. If we see a fellow slip and fall and maybe break his leg, why that's a yell to us, or his hat blow off and he cant get it.

28. There is no country in the world where a person changes from a hero to a goat and a goat to a hero, or visa versa—as they do with us. And all through no change of them, the change is always in us. It's not our public men that you cant put your finger on, it's our public. We are the only fleas weighing over 100 pounds. We dont know what we want, but we are ready to bite somebody to get it.

29. With the human race you may just as well throw your register book in the creek for what mating brings forth. No human can guess much less be certain of.

You are just as liable to bring forth a family of nuts as to produce an amateur Lincoln. Humans, it's just a name and has practically no significance at all.

30. That's what makes us a great country. The little things are serious and the big ones are not.

31. *Re* Senate investigations:

Everybody wants to hear accusations and nobody wants to hear denials.

32. The American people would trade ten investigations for one conviction.

33. We changed with the times, so we cant blame the children for just joining the times without even having to change.

34. Something ought to be done about these "Primitive" people who live in various parts of the world, and dont know a thing but to live off what nature provides. You would think they would get civilized and learn to live off each other like us civilized folks do.

33

35. [When Queen Marie of Romania visited America] it took two weeks to coach New York politicians how to dress and act to meet the Queen, so they all looked like twins and spoke the same little piece. Americans are getting like a Ford car. They all have the same parts, the same upholstering and make exactly the same noises.

36. A liberal is a man who wants to use his own ideas on things in preference to generations who he knows know more than he does.

37. I'll tell you about temperament—temperament is liable to arrive with a little success especially if you havent been used to success. The best cure for temperament is hunger. I have never seen a poor temperamental person.

38. This country is not where it is today on account of any one man. It is here on account of the real common sense of the Big Normal Majority.

39. Why anybody cant act the same away from home and enjoy just as much freedom as they do there, is more than I will ever know.

34

40. They have seen the Boragzzi Galleries [Borghese Gallery] and the Louvre, but they think the Smithsonian Institute is a clinic and the Field Museum is a branch of the great department store.

41. All Americans are wired for sound and before they go abroad they ought to detach the wiring.

42. It's always popular when in a foreign country to boost it to the detriment of your own country. You want to be sure that what you say is not going to reach back home, because after, its the home folks that count.

43. It's the Americans, or it's the American in any country that cause the Ambassador or Minister or Consul all the trouble. There is more renegade Americans abroad than there is at home.

The U.S. Government

44. We been staggering along now about 155 years under every conceivable horse-thief that could get into office and yet here we are, still going strong. I doubt if Barnum's circus has housed as many different kinds of species as has been in our government employ during its existence. As bad as they are they can't spoil

35

it, and as good as they are they can't help it. So as
bad as we are, we are better off than any other nation,
so what's the use to worry?

45. People dont change under Governments; the Governments change but the people remain the same.

46. If we could just send the same bunch of men to Washington for the good of the nation and not for political reasons, we could have the most perfect government in the world.

47. Why dont we let people alone and quit trying to hold what they call a protectorate over them? Let people do their own way and have their own form of government. We havent got any business in the Phillippines. We are not such a howling success of running our own government.

48. If people had anything to do with nominations personally, instead of it being done by half dozen men in the back rooms of some hotel, America would be a Democracy.

49. The Government has never been accused of being a business man.

50. This running a Government is kinder like our movie business. You are only as good as your last picture. Things over which they have no control comes along and yet if it happens and its bad, why out you go.

51. Course the way we do things, always have done things and will always do things, there just has to be so much graft. We wouldent feel good if there wasent. We just have to get used to charging so much off to graft just like you charge off so much for insurance, taxes or depreciation. It's a part of our national existence that we have just become accustomed to.

52. Nowadays its about as big a crime to be dumb as it is [to be] dishonest.

53. Lord, the money we do spend on Government and it's not one bit better than the government we got for one third the money twenty years ago.

54. As our Government deteriorates our humor increases.

55. If we dident have to stop and play politics any administration could almost make a Garden of Eden

out of us. You could transfer the Senate and Congress over to run the Standard Oil, or General Motors and they would have both things backrupt in two years. They are great guys personally and they know in their own heart that it's all a lot of "baloney" and if they are smart enough to make us feed 'em, why then we are the yaps, not them.

56. The Government has not only hundreds but literally thousands in Washington to see that no man can personally tend to his own business. They go there to do it for him and a mob always gets panicky quicker than an individual.

57. We will never get anywhere with our finances till we pass a law saying that every time we appropriate something we got to pass another bill along with it stating where the money is coming from.

58. Germany has a custom where they allow you to commit suicide in case you have been against the government. Over here we just let you go on making speeches and it amounts to about the same thing in the end.

59. There is no dishonesty in government. If there is,

let's dont dig it up. That's what made our government
is our faith in it.

60. No one is going to spoil the country but the people.
No one man can do it and all the people are not going to do it, so its going to run in spite of all the mis-
takes that can happen to it.

61. Always remember this, that as bad as we sometimes
think our government is run, it's the best run I ever
saw.

62. We have killed more people celebrating our Independence Day than we lost fighting for it.

63. When we got our [Independence] if history aint an
awful liar, we sure wasent in much shape to handle it.

64. That liberty that we got 159 years ago Thursday was
a great thing, but they ought to pass a law that we
could only celebrate it every 100 years, for at the rate
of accidents yesterday, we wont have enough people
to celebrate it every year. And the speeches! Did

you read them? Never was as much politics indulged in under the guise of freedom and liberty.

They was 5% what George Washington did, and 95% what the speaker intended to do. What this country needs on July the fourth is not more "liberty" or more "Freedom" it's a Roman candle that only shoots out of one end.

65. Certainly lucky for us we got our liberty when we did.

66. What might be one classes "liberty" might be another classes "poison." Course, I guess absolute "Liberty" couldent mean anything but that anybody can do anything they want to do any time they want to. Well any half-wit can tell that wouldent work. So the question rises "How much liberty can you get and get away with it?" *Well, you can get no more than you give.* That's my definition, but you got perfect "Liberty" to work out your own, so get it.

67. Liberty dont work as good in practice as it does in speeches.

Clem Vann Rogers (1839-1911), Will Rogers' father, rancher, cattleman, banker, judge of Cooweescoowee District.

Will Rogers' birthplace near Oologah,
Oklahoma, about twelve miles from
Claremore.

42

43

Will Rogers at about
the age of twelve years.

Will (seated) with
two school friends.

As a young man, Will liked to dress up and attend social functions.

Will Rogers on furlough from Kemper Military Academy, 1898.

In his early twenties Will could dance the best cake-walk in the Cherokee Nation.

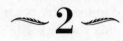

POLITICS

Politics was an inexhaustible source of subject matter for Will Rogers. In his early stage career as a rope artist, he began his monologue "I see by the papers," and in a shy, hesitant manner proceeded to comment on the current issues of the day. His deductions were so accurate that he easily earned the title of "Cowboy Philosopher."

When Will began writing for the newspapers in December 1922, he reached a class of people entirely different from theater audiences. These people avidly read his articles on the ever-changing political scene. As he toured the country on his lecture tours, he broadened his own horizon and endeared himself to people all over the United States.

The early 1920's did not have the efficient and rapid news facilities we use today, and there were many people then who did not understand the complexities of national and international politics. What they did read was not always clear to them. But when Will spoke or wrote in his good-natured, rambling style, in a language that all could understand, they welcomed his commonsense philosophy. They laughed over and agreed with his barbs at the absurdities of government policies and legislation. He became a sort of talisman for the American people; their interpreter, their spokesman and their champion.

He turned up at every presidential convention, both Democratic and Republican, to record the events for his public in a style quite unlike any other writer in the press box. He told the people the intimate things they wanted to know, yet beneath the fun he poked at the proceedings, there was a clear understanding of the political situation.

"Washington is really a merry-go-round,"[1] he declared long before Drew Pearson took such a title for his syndicated articles. No one knew this better than Will, who dodged in and out of the nation's capital, visiting the known and unknown politicians and attending functions with Washington's society leaders. He spoke and wrote what was in his mind, regardless of the consequences, though he was careful to point out the fallacies of partisan politics—a trait that made him much loved by the people and much feared by the professional politician.

He explained:

> I generally give the party in power, whether Republican or Democratic, the more digs because they are generally doing the country the most damage, and besides, I don't think it's fair to jump too much on the fellow that is down. He is not working, he is only living in hopes of getting back in on the graft in another four years, while the party in power is drawing a salary to be knocked.[2]

After Will spoke to the newspaper editors and publishers of California at Woodland in January 1933, the editor of the *Woodland Daily Democrat* commented:

> Believe it or not, Will Rogers, the cowboy funster and the man who has probably influenced more

1 Weekly article, May 14, 1933.
2 Weekly article, November 9, 1924.

48

ballots than any other living individual, has never voted. He told us so last Saturday and we believe he was serious about it. "Nope, if this here country goes to the bow-wows, there ain't no one can blame me for it," he explained. "I keep saying I'm a Democrat, but I ain't. I just pretend to be 'cause Democrats are funny and I'm supposed to be.

"Why, I travel all over the world purposely to get firsthand facts and all the inside information I can. I don't think anyone can joke intelligently unless he has something of fact to back up his humor. I have always maintained that no President can be as bad as the men that advise him."[3]

There was considerable complaint on the Rogers' quips with regard to the election of Franklin D. Roosevelt (versus Hoover) in 1932. Will was quick to defend his position:

Everybody sure was "jumpy" during this late uprising. They had a vote in their pocket and a chip on their shoulder and any insinuation made against their hero was just too bad for you. If they would just stop to think, I have written on nothing but politics for years. You never heard me on a mother-in-law joke. It was always our national and international affairs. I have been in almost every country in the last few years. I have talked with prominent men of those countries, our ambassadors, or ministers, and I would be pretty dumb not to soak up some information.

3 *Woodland* [California] *Daily Democrat,* January 26, 1933.

Now I read politics, talk politics, know personally almost every prominent politician; like 'em and they are my friends, but I can't help it if I have seen enough of it to know there is some baloney in it. I am going to be like an umpire or referee. I am going to keep on doing the same as I have in the past. I am going to call 'em as I see 'em. If I don't see things your way, well, why should I? I hope I never get so old that I can't peep behind the scenes and see the amount of politics that is mixed in this medicine before it's dished out to the people as pure statesmanship. Politics is the best show in America and I am going to keep on enjoying it.[4]

And that is what Will Rogers did. From the time he established himself as an entertainer, he seldom made a speech without bringing in something of the political situation. In the sixteen or more years he wrote for the press, he devoted much of his space to politics.

Politicians

1. Slogan: "Be a politician; no training necessary."

2. A politician is not as narrow-minded as he forces himself to be.

3. A man's thoughts are naturally on his next term more than his country.

4 Weekly article, December 18, 1932.

4. Cattlemen made the country, but it takes a politician to spoil it.

5. The more I see of politics, the more I wonder what any man would ever take it up for. Then people wonder why the best men of a community are not office holders.

6. If some efficiency expert would work out a scheme where each would be paid according to his ability, I think we would save a lot of money. Once a man holds a public office he is *absolutely no good for honest work*.

7. A king is sorta like a politician. It's hard to tell when he is making good or bad.

8. Nothing as short-sighted as a politician unless it's a delegation of them. They can ruin you quicker than unseasonable weather.

9. [Politicians] can do more funny things naturally than I can think of to do purposely.

51

10. Denounced and redenounced. That's what makes politics such a high-class gentlemanly game. Prizefighters meet and fight.

11. All legislation is put through by the aid of swaps and trades. They are just a lot of horse-traders.

12. What you say for humanity dont have near the appeal as what you say for political purposes.

13. You cant beat an administration by attacking it. You have to show some plan of improving it.

14. When you are in politics and depending on somebody to keep you in, why you really aint able to act like real life. Politicians will use any means to get their cause launched; a funeral, or a commemoration or a christening, any occasion that looks important, they will decide to launch along with the chaplain's benediction some of the promises the future holds for you.

15. It's awful hard to get people interested in corruption unless they can get some of it. Promise something in return for something whether it is a post office or an oil well.

16. Everybody that is in wants to stay in, and everybody that is out wants to get in. You know that is just what is the trouble with politics . . . there is not enough jobs to go around. You have a good job for every man and that will be the salvation of politics. You will never hear a kick. I am advocating putting into the platform "A job with every vote." If you vote for the government why not work for the government? It's harder to work for the government than it is to vote for it. In fact most jobs is not as hard.

17. Every time we have an election, we get in worse men and the country keeps right on going. Times have proven only one thing and that is you cant ruin this country ever, with politics.

18. It's not the men so much as it is the system. It just looks like they cant get away from it. Every move they take, every step they make, is with some political object in view.

19. Common sense is not an issue in politics; it's an affliction.

20. Abolish salaries and you will abolish politics and taxes.

21. There is no other business in the world that allows a man to work after he is fired except politics.

22. Nobody wants his cause near as bad as he wants to talk about his cause.

23. Everybody figures politics according to what they have accumulated during the last couple of years. Every guy looks in his pockets and then votes.

24. [Truth serum] would ruin the very foundation on which our political government is run. If you ever injected truth into politics, you would have no politics.

25. Politics hits a country like a pestilence. Somebody is going to make some money out of politics this year besides the politicians.

26. You cant believe a thing you read in regard to official's statements. The minute anything happens connected with official life, it's just like a cold night, everybody is trying to cover up.

27. Wherever you find poor soil, you will always find politics.

28. There is no more independence in politics than there is in jail. They are always yapping about "public service." It's public jobs they are looking for.

29. You can't legislate intelligence and common sense into people.

30. When a man goes in for politics over here he has no time to labor, and any man that labors has no time to fool with politics. Over there [England] politics is an obligation; over here it's a business.

31. We got the most thorough training in every line of business but statesmanship, and for that you just decide over night, "I am a statesman."

32. You come in there [as Secretary of State] labeled as a Statesman and limp out headed for the ash-can of political hopes.

33. The funny part about it [the London Conference] is that all those statesmen really thought they were going to "make History." Well, history makes itself, and the statesmen just drag along.

34. No other business in the world could afford to carry such dead wood. But we got 'em and they are going to live off us someway, so we just as well put long-tail coats on 'em and call 'em Statesmen.

35. Lobbyists in Washington are reaping a harvest. A Lobbyist is a person that is supposed to help a politician to make up his mind, not only help him, but pay him.

36. [Party politics] will never be changed because you cant change human nature. You cant broaden a man's vision if he wasent born with one.

37. Party politics is the most narrow-minded occupation in the world. A guy raised in a straight jacket is a corkscrew compared to a thick-headed politician.

38. If we dident have two parties, we would all settle on the best men in the country and things would run fine. But as it is, we settle on the worst ones and then fight over 'em.

39. It ain't much relief to just transfer your debts from

one party to another adding a little more in the bargain.

40. If a man could tell the difference between the two parties he would make a sucker of Solomon for wisdom. This country runs in spite of parties; in fact parties are the biggest handicaps we have to contend with.

Democrats

41. That's one peculiar thing about a Democrat—he would rather be told that he is right, even if he knows the guy is a liar, than he would to know he is wrong but belongs to the Republican party.

42. If the Democrats never split in their lives there would be no such thing as a Republican.

43. A Democrat never adjourns. He is born, becomes of voting age and starts right in arguing over something, and his political adjournment is his date with the undertaker. Politics is business with the Democrat. He don't work at it, but he tells what he would do if he was working at it.

44. When hungry and can't manage to get anything to

eat, [a Democrat] can always satisfy his hunger by dreaming and barking back to "Old Jeffersonian principles." Nobody knows what they were, but they have furnished a topic for the poor "Democrats" to rave about for a couple of generations.

45. Always excitement at a Democratic anything. There is always something that will stir up an argument even if they all agree.

46. A cannibal is a good deal like a Democrat, they are forced to live off each other.

Republicans

47. Republicans . . . take care of the big money, for big money takes care of them.

48. There aint any finer folks living than a Republican that votes the Democratic ticket.

49. Nothing, not even bad food, can ruin a Democratic dinner like some Republican sneaking in.

50. There must be something the matter with a Souther-

ner that would be a Republican as they are naturally
in the observation ward at all times.

51. The slaves got their freedom by war and the Republicans got theirs by secession from old Virginia.

52. Prosperity dont divide the two parties, for under
either administration, the poor get poorer and the
rich get richer. Prosperity is only a question of giving a guy time to get it. So the whole thing, it looks
like, goes back to the Civil War. The boys are still
fighting it and dont know it. They fought each other
in '65 so that made one a Democrat and one a Republican.

53. A flock of Democrats will replace a mess of Republicans. It won't mean a thing. They will go in like
all the rest of 'em. Go in on promises and come out
on alibis.

54. Split the post office jobs 50-50 and you will have a
united Democracy and a united Republicanism.

55. It takes nerve to be a Democrat, but it takes money
to be a Republican.

56. I guess the truth can hurt you worse in an election than about anything that could happen to you.

57. Political elections . . . are a good deal like marriages, there's no accounting for anyone's taste.

58. Elections . . . are like *mosquitoes,* you can't very well fight 'em off without cussing 'em.

59. I would rather have two friends in the counting room than a Republican slush fund behind me. More candidates have been defeated after six o'clock in the evening than were ever defeated during election day.

United States Senate and Senators

60. There is nothing in the world as alike as two Senators. No matter how different their politics, how different the parts of the country they come from, they all look alike, think alike and want alike. They are all looking for an appointment for some guy who helped them get theirs.

61. Most all new Senators are earnest and mean well.

Then the air of Washington gets into their bones and they are just as bad as the rest.

62. It must be nice to belong to some legislative body and just pick money out of the air.

63. There is no race of people in the world that can compete with a Senator for talking. If I went to the Senate I couldn't talk fast enough to answer roll call.

64. The United States Senate may not be the most refined and deliberative body in existence but they got the most unique rules. There ought to be one day a year when there is open session on Senators. The Constitution protects aliens, drunks and U. S. Senators.

65. All Senators travel a lot. They all try and keep away from home as much as they can.

66. I like to make little jokes and kid about the Senators. They are a never-ending source of amusement, amazement and discouragement. But the rascals, when you meet 'em they are mighty nice fellows. It must be

something in the office that makes 'em so honery sometimes. When you see what they do officially, you want to shoot 'em, but when one looks at you and grins so innocently, you kinder want to kiss him.

67. When a Gentleman quoted me on the floor the other day, another member took exception and said he objected to the remarks of a Professional Joke-Maker going into the Congressional Record.

Now can you beat that for jealousy among people in the same line? Calling me a Professional Joke Maker! He is right about everything but the Professional. They are the professional Joke Makers. I could study all my life and not think up half the amount of funny things they can think of in one Session of Congress. Besides my jokes don't do anybody any harm. You don't have to pay any attention to them. *But every one of the jokes those birds make is a law and hurts somebody,* generally everybody.

68. Who wants more congressmen? They seem to think the more we have the more loot we will get from the National Treasury in the way of appropriations. There ain't much quality in numbers.

69. I joke about 'em [Congressmen] but at heart I really like the rascals. They are all right. If one wants to

do right, our political system is so arranged that he can't do it. Mighty few retire rich, so there must be a lot more honesty about them than we give 'em credit.

Diplomats

70. Diplomats are just as essential to starting a war as Soldiers are for finishing it.

You take Diplomacy out of war and the thing would fall flat in a week. Diplomats write notes because they wouldent have the nerve to tell the same thing to each other's face.

A Diplomatic note is like an anonymous letter. You can call a fellow anything you want, for nobody can find out exactly who's name was signed to it.

71. Even a coward can be diplomatic.

72. There's one thing no nation can ever accuse us of and that's Secret diplomacy. Our foreign dealings are an open book . . . generally a check book.

73. Diplomats have a thing they call diplomatic language. It's just a lot of words and when they are all added

63

up, they don't mean a thing. On account of the President [Roosevelt] having something to say, and wanting to say it, there is no diplomatic language for that. A diplomatic language has a hundred ways of saying nothing but no way of saying something. Because he has never had anything to say, that's why they call 'em diplomats.

74. England has been the Daddy of the Diplomat, the one with the smooth manners. . . . That's one thing about an Englishman, he can insult you, but he can do it so slick and polite that he will have you guessing till way after he leaves you just whether he was a friend or foe.

75. The higher up our officials get, the less they seem to know about human nature or how to deal square with nations the same as they would with individuals.

76. A diplomat is a fellow to keep you from settling on a thing so everybody can understand it.

77. That's called diplomacy, doing just what you said you wouldent.

BUSINESS,

THE LAW AND LAWYERS

Will Rogers loved people. As he traveled over the country he visited with the big and little businessmen "To get their angle, as to how things were going." In this manner he gained an astounding knowledge of the business structure of the nation.

In his own business dealings he had an uncanny insight that he called "hunches." He employed no agent, and he had no adviser; but as calls for the stage, screen, radio and writing came to him, he would deliberate over these opportunities, toss some aside and wait until the prompting hunch presented itself. Fortunately, this led him into the proper channels as he climbed steadily in his craft. He held to the old-fashioned idea that a man's word was his bond; a contract meant nothing to him. "Advice," he said, "can get you in more trouble than a gun can. I don't want somebody telling me how to run my business or my country."[1]

While he numbered among his friends some of the greatest financial men of the time, he was never known

[1] Weekly article, August 20, 1933.

to use this friendship to benefit himself or take advantage of a situation at the expense of another. He took no chances on the stock market, explaining: "I never in my life made a single dollar without having to chew some gum to get it."[2] He played a lone game in the world of business and accepted no binding obligations.

He felt that money was for spending and giving. He bought unlimited happiness and comfort for others. As his fortune increased, so did his giving. No one demonstrated the share-the-wealth plan more bountifully than Will Rogers.

Business

1. A country is known by its strength, and a man by his check book.

2. The old community spirit waves just so long as everybody is collecting.

3. The day of the guy working for himself is past. We are living in an age of "Mergers." When your business is not doing good you combine with something and sell more stock. The poor little fellow, he can't combine with anything but the sheriff in case he is going broke. But "big business" merges with another that's not going good and both do "nothing" together.

2 Weekly article, November 10, 1929.

One of the weaknesses of the American people is that if two things go together they think it must be great.

4. In no business is a man entitled to more than he can draw and every man is entitled to a fair share of every cent he can draw.

5. There is nothing that can break a man quicker than land, unless it's running a grocery store or dealing in second-hand cars.

6. Samuel Gompers has spent his life trying to keep labor from working too hard and he has succeeded beyond his own dreams.

7. I tell you everybody ought to have two or three things they work at; and then when one busts, they got the others.

8. It's not what you pay a man but what he costs you that counts.

9. Half the people in the U.S. are living on interest paid

by people who will never get the last mortgage paid.

10. People that pay for things never complain. It's the guy you give something to that you cant please.

11. A debt is just as hard for a government to pay as an individual. No debt ever came due at a good time. Borrowing is the only thing that is handy all the time.

12. We will never get things really righted in our country till every line of sport, industry, profession or trade have some system of everyone contributing while working to the welfare of the old and unemployed in his own line. I dont mean to put all ball players in an old ball-player's home, I mean a system of help where it's done and they retain their respect and courage and self-esteem.

13. A guy [Saunders] in Memphis that started this Piggly Wiggly business, he figured that if somebody give you a basket and told you to go to it, that you would take more junk than if somebody was digging it out for you. The Woman instinct would naturally make her believe that the fellow looking in the bag at the finish might overlook something.

14. One third of the people in the U.S. promote, while the other two thirds provide.

15. Shrewdness in public life all over the world is always honored while honesty in public men is generally attributed to dumbness and seldom rewarded.

16. There is men in business that don't belong in business any more than the government does and that's why the government has to go in.

17. That's all America is, a business institution.

18. The difference between doing a thing for money and doing it for nothing makes it legal.

19. Our problem is not what is the dollar worth in London, Rome, or Paris, or what even it is worth at home. It's how to get hold of it, whatever its worth.

20. The old dollar might be filthy lucre, but there is

quite a bit of energy and spirit yet in earning one.

21. Big business sure got big, but it got big by selling its stocks and not by selling its products. No scheme was halted by the government as long as somebody would buy the stock.

22. The Stock Market has spoiled more appetites than bad cooking.

23. Wall Street has gone into one tail-spin after another. If it kept on like this it would discourage gambling— that would be bad for the country.

24. They always did say the heart of the American people was sound. In fact, it was sounder than most of the stocks that the sound heart bought.

25. Insurance companies have guys figure the very day you will die. (In fact, they won't insure till they have investigated and find out.) Then you, like a sucker, go bet them you will live longer than that.

26. Lloyds of London . . . will bet with you on anything and let you take either side you want.

27. Fireproofing and insurance have caused more fires than going to bed with a lighted cigarette.

28. The same fellows make them [insurance and political platforms] out. What they say on one page, they can deny on the other.

29. Our country has got so that each one of us has to live by a "racket" of some kind, and none of us must be too critical of the other fellow's racket.

Law and Lawyers

30. Everytime a lawyer writes something, he is not writing for posterity, he is writing so that endless others of his craft can make a living out of trying to figure out what he said. Course perhaps he hadent really said anything, that's what makes it hard to explain.

31. The minute you read something and you cant understand it, you can almost be sure that it was drawn up

by a lawyer. Then if you give it to another lawyer to read and he dont know just what it means, why then you can be sure it was drawn up by a lawyer. If it's in a few words and is plain and understandable only one way, it was written by a non-lawyer.

32. *Re* corruption in politics:

It's what lawyers call "sharp practice." So it's going to be awful hard to make an issue of corruption.

33. That's one thing about these politicians, when they cant make politics pay, they can always fall back on the honest profession of *Law*.

34. A man dont any more learn where the ice box is in the White House than he has to go back to being a lawyer again.

35. Just addressed the California State Legislature and helped them pass a bill to form a Lawyers' Association to regulate their conduct. Personally, I dont think you can make a lawyer honest by an act of legislature. You've got to work on his conscience and his lack of conscience is what makes him a lawyer.

72

36. I have always noticed that anytime a man cant come and settle with you without bringing his lawyer, why look out for him.

37. Diplomats are nothing but high class lawyers. Some aint even high class.

38. Here is about the best crime prevention news I have seen. "The California Bar Association is to rid its ranks of any attorney found to have connection with the underworld."

    The first thing they do now, if they are taking up crime as a profession (even before they buy the gun) is to engage their lawyer. He works on a percentage. He acts as their advance agent, too. He picks out the banks they are to rob. The Bar Association invented the word "ethics," then forgot it.

39. You almost have to be a lawyer in Washington to hold your own.

40. Some one suggested in case of mis-trial the Judge should hear the evidence and render the decision. What a howl the law profession put up! That was cutting right into their graft. What a justice-seeking bunch of babies they turned out to be.

41. All these laws that they are having so much trouble wondering if they are constitutional, they were all drawn up by lawyers. For almost two-thirds of the membership of the House and Senate are lawyers.

42. America has 110 million population [as of 1924], 90 per cent which are lawyers, yet we can't find two of them who have not worked at sometime or other for an oil company. *There has been at least one lawyer engaged for every barrel of oil that ever came out of the ground.*

43. Thousands of students just gradauted all over the country in Law. Going to take an awful lot of crime to support that bunch. A man naturally pulls for the business that brings him in his living. That's human nature, so look what a new gang we got to assist devilment. All trained to get a guilty man out on a technicality and an innocent one in on their opposing lawyer's mistake. This is the heyday of the shyster lawyer and they defend each other for half rates.

44. Law is complications and complications are Law. If everything was just plain, there wouldn't be any lawyers.

45. We are always saying, "Let the Law take its course."

But what we mean is "Let the Law take *our* course."

46. One level-headed smart man could interpret every law there is. If you commit a crime you did or you dident, without habeas corpus, change of venue, or any other legal shindig. But, lord, if we go into these things that are useless, why two-thirds of the world would have to turn to manual labor. That's really the only essential things there is.

47. *Re* The Legal Record:

"Dedicated to the interests of the legal profession," it's a paper that has nothing to do with news. It tells you right off we take nothing but the lawyers' side. (For there aint any other.)

48. Went down and spoke at some Lawyers' meeting last night. They dident think much of my little squib yesterday about driving the shysters out of their profession. They seemed to kinder doubt just who would have to leave.

49. If it weren't for wills, lawyers would have to work at an essential employment. There is only one way you can beat a lawyer in a death case. That is to die

with nothing. Then you cant get a lawyer within 10 miles of your house.

50. Modern history has proven that there has never yet been a will left that was carried out exactly as the maker of the money intended. So if you are thinking of dying and have any money, I would advise you to leave the following will:

"Count up the lawyers in the state and divide it among them. If there should by any miracle be any left, let my Relatives, all of them, God bless 'em, fight over it."

51. By all means leave a will. Leave a will so the lawyers can misinterpret what you meant when you knew enough to know what you wanted to do with your money.

Will Rogers about 1905 on his trick pony, "Teddy," named for
Theodore Roosevelt.

77

Betty (Mrs. Will) Rogers and "Teddy," about 1909.

Will Rogers on "Dopey," one of his roping horses, at his Long Island place, about 1916, when he was appearing in the *Follies*.

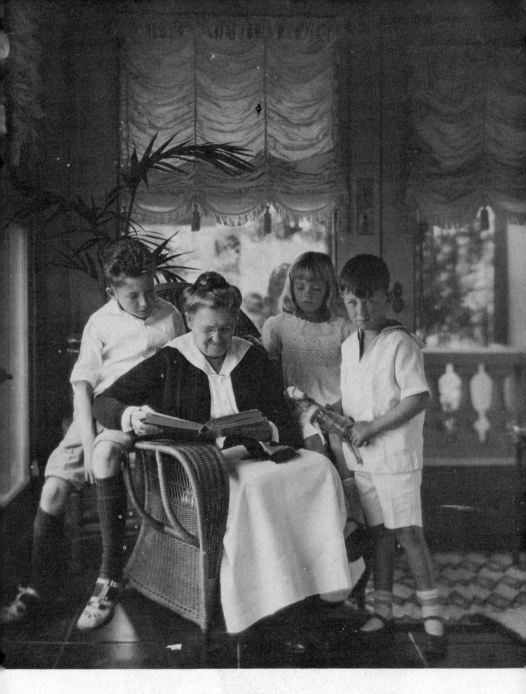

"Mamoo" Blake, mother of Mrs. Will Rogers, with the Rogers' children, Bill, Jim and Mary, at their Beverly Hills home about 1920.

The Rogers family about 1922, when they were living on Long Island, N.Y., and Will was in the *Follies*. Jimmie is in the front seat with his father; Mrs. Rogers is in the back seat with Mary and Will, Jr.

Mr. and Mrs. Rogers returning from a round-the-world trip, Sept. 1934.

WR-17

Will and Betty Rogers, 1928.

The Rogers family polo team at their Santa Monica, California, ranch,

about 1930. From *left to right*: Jimmie, Mary, Will, Jr., Will Rogers.

4

BANKERS AND TAXES

During the last years of his life in Claremore, Oklahoma, Will's father was a banker. He was a generous-hearted man, affectionately called "Uncle Clem," who helped many of the early-day citizens get started in business and also kept a host of others from financial ruin and the poor house.

Naturally, Will had a great respect for bankers as a whole, but he did not always approve of the way some of them transacted business. Because he was free with his own money and tried to do all he could to help the unfortunates, it was difficult for him to understand why the banker was not more lenient. He had seen the result of the drought in the Southwest when he toured the country on his own relief drive, and felt that some of the most deserving people were entirely overlooked.

The years following the crash of the stock market were some of the most crucial in the banking industry. This was a timely topic for Will, who noted these events in his role as a humorist.

He was a popular speaker at bankers' meetings and conventions and often addressed the bankers as "Loan-Sharks! Shylocks! Skinflints! The greatest bunch of men that ever foreclosed a mortgage on a widow's home."

The bankers laughed spontaneously at his remarks, for each one knew Will was not referring to him, but to the other fellow.

Under the guise of this good-natured banter, Will could drive a point home like a guided missile. As he chose to defend the class of people who were not able to speak for themselves, he usually put himself also on the defensive. In speaking of his holding in this connection he wrote:

> We call 'em ranches in California. It sounds big and dont cost any more on the lien. Mine is called "Rancho Premire y Segundo Mortgages." The literal translation of that is the "Ranch of the First and Second Mortgages," and there would be a third if these old bankers were more liberal minded.[1]

Bankers

1. There are more [bankers] in Ossining[2], N. Y., than any town its size in the United States.

2. Show me ten men that mortgage their land to get money and I will have to get a search warrant to find one that gets the land back again. If you think it aint a sucker game, why is your banker the richest man in your town?

Let 'em go to work, if there is any job any of them

1 Weekly article, September 17, 1933.
2 Sing Sing Prison is in Ossining.

could earn a living at. Banking and after-dinner speaking are two of the most nonessential industries we have in this country. I am ready to reform if they are.

3. I saw one of their [American Legion] conventions and they act almost half as bad as the American Bankers' Association, who had nothing to celebrate but foreclosed mortgages.

4. All newsboys become politicians and all bootblacks become bankers.

5. An old country boy banker from Colorado slicked the city-slicker bankers out of one-half million bucks and they give him fifteen years so fast that you would have thought he had assassinated a big government official. You let a city bank slick an old country boy out of something and before night he will merge with another bank and finally wind up as a member of the Federal Reserve.

6. There is no such thing as a little bootlegger, no more than there is a little banker. The day of the little banker in a small town is past. He is a member of a chain. He is a subsidiary of some big concern.

86

7. Is there any way of checking up on a bank president or vice-president to see what he can actually by his own efforts draw into his bank?

8. If a bank fails in China, they behead the men at the the head of it that was responsible. If one fails over here, we write the men up in the magazines, as how they started poor, worked hard, took advantage of their opportunities (and depositors) and today they are rated up in the millions.

9. There is nothing as scary as a banker. He dont wait for the grave yard to whistle, he will do it passing a hearse.

10. Our home bankers, both large and small, are in bad just thru the bad times and an over expansion in good times, but the International one is in bad thru malice aforethought. His devilment was premeditated. He knew he was loaning on no security in Europe, cause there is no security over there. He got his commissions for peddling it out so what does he care.

11. You know, there is nothing as tiring and boring in this country as just a rich man. So my scheme is to bring 'em back to respectability. I am going to start with

87

the bankers. If I can make Bankers loved by the community again, it is going to be a God-send to their families.

12. The Banker, the Lawyer, and the Politician are still our best bets for a laugh. Audiences havent changed at all, and neither has the three above professions.

Taxes

13. I see a great deal of talk from Washington about lowering the taxes. I hope they get 'em lowered down enough so people can afford to pay 'em.

14. Alexander Hamilton originated the "put and take" system into our national treasury. The tax payers put it in and the politicians take it out.

15. Every statesman wants to vote appropriations but is afraid to vote taxes.

16. Everybody is on a trip somewhere if they work for the Government. I wonder when the taxpayers take their trip.

17. When a party cant think of anything else they always fall back on lower taxes, but no voter has lived to see the day when his taxes were lowered. Presidents have been promising lower taxes since Washington crossed the Delaware by hand in a row boat, but our taxes have gotten bigger and their boats have gotten larger until now the President crosses the Delaware in his private yacht.

18. There is dozens of great humanitarian things that could be done at a very little cost, if the tax was properly applied. It's the waste in government that gets everybody's goat.

19. Every time Congress starts to tax some particular industry it rushes down with its main men and they scare 'em out of it. About the only way I see for 'em to do it so it would be fair to everybody would be for Congress to go into secret session, allow no telephones, no telegrams, no visitors, so no outside lobbyist can get at 'em, then tax everything they should tax, then announce: "Boys, it's all over; there is no use shooting at us now." As it is now, we are taxing everybody without a lobby.

20. If we were run by the Manager form of Government we would be paying so little taxes we would be lonesome.

21. It's a great country but you cant live in it for nothing.

22. Did you ever figure it out, taxes is all there is to politics?

23. Income Tax was another issue of his [William Jennings Bryan] advocated twenty years before it was adopted. If we had started paying it then, we would have been used to it by now and it wouldent seem so hard.

24. The Income Tax has made more liars out of the American people than golf has.

25. The crime of taxation is not in the taking of it, it's in the way it's spent.

26. This is income tax paying day. There is going to be no attempt at humor for it would be mighty forced. No two can agree on what is deductable. When it's made out you dont know if you are a crook or a martyr.

27. Congress knocked the rich in the creek with a [raise

in the] income tax, then somebody must have told 'em: "Yes, Congress, you got 'em while they are living. But what if they die on you to keep from paying it?" Congress says: "Well, never thought of that so we will frame one that will get 'em alive or living, dead or deceased." Now they got such a high inheritance tax on 'em that you wont catch these old rich boys dying promiscuously like they did. This bill makes patriots out of everybody. You sure do die for your country, if you die from now on.

28. I dont see why a man shouldent pay inheritance tax. If a country is good enough to pay taxes to while you are living, it's good enough to pay in after you die. By the time you die, you should be so used to paying taxes that it would be almost second nature.

29. It aint taxes that is hurting the country; it's interest.

30. Nobody has ever invented a slogan to use instead of paying your taxes.

31. A fellow can always get over losing money in a game of chance but he seems so constituted that he can never get over money thrown away to a government in taxes. In other words he will bet on anything but he wont pay it to you in taxes.

32. People dont mind spending their money if they know it isn't going for taxes.

33. Oh, boy—where is all the money coming from that the government is throwing away? Well, it just sorter looks like it might come from the ones that have got it. There is one good thing about our American form of government—the fellow that's got nothing, pays nothing; and too, lots of times the fellow that's got something, but nothing to pay with. But he can at least let 'em have the property and break even. But the big yell comes nowadays from the taxpayers. I guess when the pilgrims landed on Plymouth Rock and they had the whole of American continent, and all they had to do to get an extra 160 acres was to shoot another Indian, I bet you anything they kicked on the price of the ammunition. I bet they said, "What's this country coming to that we have to spend a nickle for powder?" Of course, they got the lead back after they dissected the Indian. No matter what you pay for taxes, high or low, medium, the yell is always the same, 100 per cent.

Course we know our Government is costing us more than it's worth. But do you know of anybody that has a cheaper one? You can try Russia—there is no income tax in Russia, but there's no income.

34. [Baseball] is a skilled game. It's America's game, it and high Taxes.

35. Taxation is about all there is to government. People want just *taxes* more than they want *lower* taxes. They want to know that every man is paying his proportionate share according to his wealth.

36. Incidentally comedians havent improved. Nothing has improved but taxes.

~~5~~

PRESIDENTS

Will was considered a great power in the political world, and this fact did not go unnoticed by the Presidents of the United States. His personal acquaintance with Presidents began with Theodore Roosevelt and extended to Franklin D. Roosevelt. A man like Teddy Roosevelt, who lived and typified "the strenuous life," stirred the imagination of the young Will. While he was on the vaudeville circuit in 1905, he wrote home to his sisters from the Chase Opera House, October 30:

> Don't know if I will make the White House this trip as old Teddy aint here and young Teddy is away at school. I don't much care to as I did it once and they might think I wanted to use it for advertising purposes, but I dont know what will show up before the week is over.[1]

Will's clever pony that he used in his roping act was named "Teddy" in honor of the President, but when he played Washington, D. C., at the Gayety Theater the week of February 25, 1907, Teddy was billed as "Arcade" out of respect to the man who held the highest office in the U.S.A.

[1] Family letters, October 30, 1905.

Throughout his life Will enjoyed an intimate friendship with the Roosevelts, especially Alice Roosevelt and her husband Nicolas Longworth, U.S. Congressman from 1903 to 1931 and Speaker of the House during the Coolidge and Hoover administrations.

In an undated letter to his sister about 1915, Will tells of appearing before President Woodrow Wilson. He was in the *Follies* at this time. He wrote:

> We played to the President last night. I will write you all about it in a letter in a day or so. I joked all about the Peace Ship [Henry Ford's] going to Europe, he sure enjoyed it. I had lunch today with Mr. and Mrs. Nick Longworth at their home. Their home you could put all Rogers County in it. . . .[2]

Woodrow Wilson was one of the first to call Will Rogers a humorist when he said, "His remarks are not only humorous but illuminating."[3]

In later years Will himself had been mentioned for the Presidency with all seriousness by various groups and individuals, but he always scoffed at the idea. "I would rather tell 'em what I think and retire with satisfaction than be President and be hampered."[4]

Will was always a welcome guest at the White House and each President was glad to laugh at his jokes on the administration, or, in a serious mood, find out how conditions were in certain countries he had visited. He was indeed an unofficial ambassador of good will. His keen analysis of foreign affairs was always sought by the Chief Executive and not thrust on him.

2 Family letters.
3 Michel Mok, newspaper story, 1935.
4 Weekly article, March 4, 1934.

95

After the bitter campaign of 1932, when Will advised both Roosevelt and Hoover to go fishing and quit the name-calling, he got a number of rebukes from his readers for writing about the President. He answered them in "A Letter to the Times":

> Now I poke my little fun at the Presidents, but I don't care who you are, you havent got any more respect for the man and the office than I have. I think Mr. Hoover knows what I think of him personally and how I admire him as a man. I have never gone to Washington that I havent gone in and had a chat with him and I feel that I can again.
>
> Mr. Coolidge, who I made a living out of for years, had no greater and still has no greater admirer and staunch supporter of his splendid qualities, than I am.
>
> Now this Mr. Roosevelt that's coming in, he is a particular friend of mine for many years standing, he and his whole family, but I have got to start in now pretty soon making a living out of the fool things that he and those Democrats will do, and I am not worried, I know they will do plenty of 'em.
>
> The one thing that I am proud of is the fact that there is not a man in public life today that I dont like. Most of them are my good friends, but that's not going to keep me from taking a dig at him when he does something or says something foolish.[5]

5 *Los Angeles Times*, November 10, 1932.

Presidents in General

1. Presidents become great, but they have to be made Presidents first.

2. We have lived under over 30 Presidents. They couldn't have all been great. In fact if we told the truth about 'em, maybe some of 'em was pretty punk. But we drug along in spite of 'em.

3. No one of the whole 30 of them that we have had ever did what anyone of the others did. All of the candidates study what to do and who to do it to.

4. It don't make any difference who it is. None of them from any party are going to purposely ruin the country. They will all do the best they can.

5. You can get your name on a button easier than you can get it on the letter box in front of the White House.

6. There just seems to be something about running for President that you can never get out of a fellow's

head. He never seems to figure his chances. It can be on an "off year," or "Leap Year" and just nominate him, and he is perfectly tickled to death. That he will wind up by just being a defeated candidate never seems to enter his head. That "The Time is not ripe for it" is as foreign to his thoughts as the moon.

7. If you eliminate the names of Lincoln, Washington, Roosevelt, Jackson and Wilson, both conventions would get out three days earlier.

8. A good campaign manager can do more than an able candidate. "Trades" makes Presidents, more than ability, but as bad as we are, and as funny as we do things, we are better off than the other countries, so bring on more conventions. No Nation likes "hooey" like we do. We are all cookoo, but we are happy.

9. A guiding hand in any business now needs encouragement and especially in guiding the biggest business in the world. Lord, what a tough time to have a country on your hands.

10. The Congressmen and Senators are not supposed to know anything about the country, and they generally dont, so the President issues his message.

11. Distrust of the Senate by Presidents started with Washington who wanted to have 'em court-martialled. Jefferson proposed life imprisonment for 'em. Old Andy Jackson, said, "To Hell with 'em" and got his wish. Lincoln said, "The Lord must have hated 'em for he made so few of 'em." Roosevelt whittled a big stick and beat on 'em for six years. Taft just laughed at 'em and grew fat. They drove Wilson to an early grave. Coolidge never let 'em know what he wanted, so they never knew how to vote against him, and Mr. Hoover took 'em serious, thereby making his only political mistake.

12. Once a man is President he is just as hard to pry out of there as a Senator, or a town constable or any political office.

13. Sometimes it makes you think we dont need a different man as bad as we need different advisers for the same man.

14. No matter what a President does, he is wrong according to some people, so I couldent even say yes or no if I was him. I would just stall along and if asked I would remark, "I dont choose to answer." But take all in all, it's a tough life. This thing of being President and trying to please everybody—well, not exactly everybody, but enough to re-elect.

99

15. Course the President, he is always conceded the nomination at the next election unless he has been notoriously incompetent. But all things being as they usually are, why he of course can have the election if he wants it. And history has never recorded the one that dident. Coolidge dident but he had already had practically two terms. And there is a kind of unwritten law against that. But it wasent a third term bugaboo that kept Calvin out, it was horse sense. He knew just to an inch how much American wind the financial balloon would hold and he got out just two days before it busted. Poor Mr. Hoover dident see the thing any more than poor Rin Tin. Tin.

It was set that Mr. Hoover could have it if he chose, and he did choose, and how! They do love to be President. It's the toughest job in the world, but there is always 120 million applicants.

16. Every party and everybody must have some platform formed even if its in their minds. Mine is that a President should hold office six years with no re-election. Stop this thing of a President having to lower his dignity and go trooping around asking for votes to keep him there another term. He has to do it, naturally, but a six-year term with no re-election will be the remedy. Six years gives him time to do something. It takes him four years to find out who is his friends in the Senate and House. There is a lot of Senators in there for six years. Look at the saving of all the money, all the time, all the uncertainty of another election. It lessens it one-third.

Then pay the man when he goes out one-half of his salary for life. The country should keep an ex-President from bankruptcy if it can keep a railroad or a badly managed bank. Course the Cabinet wouldent have much to do on their last summer in office like they do now, but they could hang around their office and kill time.

George Washington

17. A Virginia planter. A farmer that needs no relief but just wants to clean the British out and figures we can run it ourselves and cut out the overhead.

18. He was the most versatile President we ever had. He was a farmer, civil engineer and a gentleman. He made enough at civil engineering to indulge in both the other luxuries.

19. He was a surveyor. He took the exact measure of the British and surveyed himself out about the most valuable piece of land in America at that time, Mount Vernon. George could not only tell the truth but land values.

20. Of course he was great. He was the Father of our

Country on account of having no children. He was a surveyor and he owned half of Virginia because he surveyed his own lines. He was a General on our side because England wouldent make him one of theirs. He was a politician and a gentleman—that is a rare combination.

21. Washington was elected the first President because he was about the only one who had enough money to give a decent inauguration party. Then every once in a while he would whip England. That wasent an accomplishment. That was a habit. He really took the job so he could locate the capital in Washington.

22. Originally in our country the Government owned all the land there was outside the original 13 colonies and England owned that. Then Washington had a war and took it away from them and annexed most of it personally himself. What he dident get, a Democrat named Jefferson got.

23. [The Capital] was really the first real estate promotion scheme; Washington and Jefferson owned practically all the land down that way, and geographical reasons had nothing to do with locating the capital there. It wasent the center of the country, but it was the center of George's and Tom's land holdings. So while you dident get much money for

being President in those days, it wasent exactly a philanthropic job. George lost no money through the transaction. He and Jefferson landed on two of the best hills in that country, and the Government got the swamps.

24. Even in the beginning when George Washington run against himself there must have been some little issue that the voters could be pro or con over. Even if it was over whether he should bob his wig or just over the white horse he used to have his picture painted on.

25. It's been fairly well established that Washington slept here [Philadelphia] in not only one but various beds. Washington crossed the Delaware (with everybody rowing but him). I don't remember whether he crossed it to get to or away from Philadelphia.

26. Washington . . . fought for his tribe against the invaders [Indians] and wound up with a flock of statutes and a title of Father-of-His-Country. I expect if the truth were known, the old Apache Chiefs went through more and fought harder for their country than George did. But George won, that's the whole answer to history. It's not what did you do, but what did you get away with at the finish.

27. All we seem to celebrate Washington's Birthday for is so we can revive the argument as to "what he had to say about entanglements with Europe." Every speaker makes him say just what that speaker wants him to say. Coolidge says it was Jefferson that made the "wise crack" about not messing with outsiders. So, it looks like added to all his other accomplishments Washington was a diplomat.

Thomas Jefferson

28. He was the most far-sighted Democrat in either his or any other time and they named the Democratic party after him. That is he was for the poor but was himself of the rich.

29. Jefferson sitting up there on that hill believed in equality for all. But he dident divide up that hill with any poor Democrats. (For Democrats were poor in those days as they are today.)

30. Jefferson seemed to be the only Democrat in history with any kind of business ability.

31. They havent had a man that rode a horse to the White House since Jefferson.

32. There's a lad that never missed a shot or a drink while he was in the White House.

33. Course I knew what a great man he had been but at the same time I had heard enough to know that an "Injun" dident exactly rate high with him. I knew he had a lot to do with running the Cherokees out and making them go West, but I knew he had unconsciously favored us in the long run so I forgave him.

34. He is the one that run us Cherokees out of Georgia and North Carolina. I ate the [Jackson Day] dinner on him, but I dident enjoy it. I thought I was eating for Stonewall. Old Andy, every time he couldent find any one to jump on, would come back and pounce onto us Indians. Course he licked the English down in New Orleans, but he dident do it till the war had been over two weeks, so he really just fought them as an encore. Then he would have a row with the Government and they would take his command and his liquor away from him and he would come back and sick himself onto us Cherokees again.

He was the first one to think up the idea to promise everybody that if they will vote for you, you will give them an office when you get it, and the more times they vote for you, the bigger the office. But old Andy made the White House. He got in before the Republicans got their scheme working. The Indians wanted him in there so he would let us alone for awhile. Andy stayed two terms and was the first man that dident "Choose to run" again. He had to get back to his regular business which was shooting at the Indians.

35. He fought duels when duels was duels and not just the inconvenience of getting up before sunrise.

36. About all old Andrew was responsible for was the system that made us all have to sit there and listen to such junk [speeches]. Andrew was the one that said, "If you dont get out and work for the party you don't get in on the gravy after election."

37. [Jackson] brought undying fame to the glorious state of Tennessee. He did it by personal bravery and unmatched intelligence.

Abraham Lincoln

38. Honest Abe wasent hardly a bottle fed baby all through life. Even if he dident split all those rails, just piling up rails after somebody else had split 'em is hardly child's play.

39. I dont know what the particular issue was in Lincoln's election but you can bet as good an axeman as he was he had some kind of a clean cut issue.

40. Is there anybody here [Princeton University] teaches reading or writing or arithmetic or some of the old fashioned things Lincoln struggled along with to Presidency?

41. If Abe Lincoln from Illinois was resurrected and was to fill out this unexpired term and he still insisted he was a Republican, there would be a party vote against him.

42. They dug up another monument or repainted an old one or something over in Illinois. This was to Abraham Lincoln, another Republican. Hoover said: "Get 'em all dedicated on one trip."

43. If it hadent been for Lincoln, the Republicans in N.Y. would sure be short of a cause for celebrating.

44. Some man . . . from Illinois got up to nominate somebody [at the Democratic Convention of 1924] and

we knew we would hear something about Lincoln being born in Illinois. He kept quoting Lincoln's famous remark about "God must have loved the common people because he made so many of them." You are not going to get people's votes nowadays by calling them common. Lincoln might have said it, but I bet it was not until he was elected.

45. The last few days I have read various addresses made on Lincoln's birthday. Every politician always talks about him, but none of them ever imitate him.

46. Lincoln was great. He freed the slaves and put the Southern whites in bondage for the duration of their natural lives. He furnished General Grant with cigars to smoke and poor Lee had no gas mask so he had to surrender. Lincoln tried his best to prevent that war between the Democrats and the Republicans. Since then, they have been settling their difficulties at the polls with about the same results.

47. Papers today say, "What would Lincoln do today?" Well, in the first place, he wouldent chop any wood, he would trade his ax in on a Ford. Being a Republican he would vote the Democratic Ticket. Being in sympathy for the under dog he would be classed as a radical progressive. Having a sense of humor he would be called eccentric.

48. Lincoln made a wonderful speech one time: "That this nation under God, shall have a new birth of freedom, and that Government of the People, by the People, for the People shall not perish from this earth." Now, every time a politician gets in a speech, he digs up this Gettysburg quotation. He recites it every Decoration Day and practices the opposite the other 364 days.

Now Mr. Lincoln meant well, but he only succeeded in supplying an applause line for every political speaker who was stuck for a finish.

49. Another Decoration Day passed and Mr. Abraham Lincoln's 300-word Gettysburg address was not dethroned. I would try to imitate its brevity if nothing else. Of course, Lincoln had the advantage. He had no foreign policy message to put over. He dident even have a foreign policy. That's why he is still Lincoln.

50. No man should ever make a speech after somebody has read or recited Lincoln's Gettysburg Address. It's only about 300 words long and the plainest words. There's not a child or even a comedian that can't understand it. Honest, Lincoln just as well not made his speech as far as it has had any effect on other speakers. He left it as an example but no one ever followed it.

He was not what is always humorously referred to as

the "Principal Speaker." And this little speech of Lincoln's dident go over so big. They all say Lincoln wrote his going up on the train in a day coach, on the back of an envelope. Every speaker that goes to commemorate something or other, should be locked up in a day-coach and if he comes out with over 300 words then he should be put in a cattle car and make it to the stock.

Theodore Roosevelt

51. Teddy Roosevelt was my best bet for a laugh in those days [vaudeville]. He was the best known public man that ever lived, and they kept up with everything that he did. So when you started in talking about something that he had just said or done, you dident have to stop and tell what it was before going ahead with your comment.

52. Teddy was a man that wouldent waste even hatred on nothing.

53. If we can spare men like Roosevelt and Wilson there is no use in any other politician ever taking himself seriously.

54. The reason I advocate electing our officials for life

is that no matter what man is in office, the one that you put in his place is worse. If we had kept our original cast that we had to start with, we would have been better off. We had no business ever letting Washington, (George, not D.C., I mean) go. We ought to have kept him till we got a hold of Lincoln, then been more careful of the protection of his life and preserved him to a ripe old age down to where [Teddy] Roosevelt was say 15 years old. Then we could have turned it over to him. He would have run it as good at that age as most men could at 50.

William Howard Taft

55. In our Decoration Day speechmaking Mr. Taft spoke at some unveiling of a monument in Cincinnati. He made an alibi for the Supreme Court. I don't know what prompted him to tell the dead what the court was doing, unless it was some man who had died of old age waiting for a decision from that august body.

56. *Re* the death of President Taft:

Mr. Taft, what a lovely old soul. Fat and good natured. All of our Presidents that his generation knew, some we felt we dident know, some we admired their ability, some we had great faith in, and all of them symbolized the great office they occupied. But just as a man, and a real honest-to-God fellow, Mr. Taft will go to his grave with more real downright affection and less enemies than any. . . . He always seemed like he was one óf us. He was our great human fellow because there was more of him to be human. We are parting with 300 pounds of solid charity to everybody, and love and affection for all his fellowmen.

Calvin Coolidge

57. [Coolidge] got so used as Vice President to have no one pay any attention to what any of them said he cant realize they might listen to him now.

58. He kept his mouth shut. That was such a novelty among politicians that it just swept the country. Originality will be rewarded in any line.

59. My campaign contributions would do credit to Calvin Coolidge as I havent spent a cent.

60. President Coolidge gave a luncheon for visiting Governors where they discussed but dident try prohibition.

61. Being great as President is not a matter of knowledge or far-sightedness. It's just a question of the weather not only in your own country but in a dozen others.

It's the elements that make you great or that break you. So, it's sorter like a World's Series—you got to have the breaks. Bad advice will ruin you just about as a total earthquake would. Every guy just looks in his pockets and then votes. And the funny part of it is it's the last year that is the one that counts. You can have three bad ones and then wind up with everybody having money, and you will win so far you needent even stay up to hear the returns. You may think you can out-general Cal, but you look up his record and you are going to have a tough time out-lucking him.

62. He knows . . . a good crop next year will do more for free rent than all the promises he could think of to make now.

63. [Coolidge] came in here with nothing but a valise and a speech on economy. Nobody begrudges him what he has been able to save up during these years and when he is up there [Vermont]. In that town there aint much to look at—only what you bring in with you.

64. Calvin wants to buy something for us but he wants Hoover to pay for it. He is more set on going out of office having his budget balanced than he is going

113

out with any other thing. We may be in a terrible lot of scrapes, but we wont be in the red.

65. Here comes Coolidge and does nothing and retires a hero, not only because he hadent done anything, but because he had done it better than anyone.

Herbert Clark Hoover

66. In 1914, he was chairman of the American Relief Association and he helped feed Belgians, and a little later it was found we was worse off than the Belgians, so they brought him home to feed us. He is always feeding somebody. Now he is feeding the Republicans. No Armenian that ever lived can eat more than one of them can.

He really won the war for us. Did you ever figure that out? He won the war for us, but he ruined our stomachs. He gave us liberty with indigestion.

67. Hoover is talking about resigning—that shows right there he is not a politician. He seems to think you cant serve two masters.

68. He has seen more of the world, (not only than any

114

President) but more than any Notre Dame football team. He has no use for politicians, which fact elected him by the largest majority ever recorded. If he will just continue to hate them we are liable to wake up with another Lincoln or Jefferson on our hands.

69. Mr. Hoover hadent been sworne in over three quarters of an hour till the desire to be President on the part of half of Mexico broke out. It looks like his being inaugurated kinder put the same idea into 34 Generals' heads in Mexico. All you had to do to be President was to shoot the one that was and that brought on some pretty fancy marksmanship. The old way of electing Presidents by the bullet instead of the ballot.

70. Mr. Hoover has done all in his power to try and further peace and at the same time leave us a musket loaded in the corner.

71. I always did want to see him elected. I wanted to see how far a competent man could go in politics. It has never been tried before.

72. We ought to have a social President. There just aint any end to what he could relieve Mr. Hoover of.

Get a man and his wife with good digestion, good disposition and a master of Emily Post.

73. [Hoover] reaped the benefits of the arrogance of the party when it was going strong.

Franklin Delano Roosevelt

74. This Roosevelt is a mighty fine human man. Sometimes I think he is too nice a fellow to be mixed up in all this politics.

75. See where the Roosevelts, even down unto the fifth cousins, are straying back into the fold. Nothing will bring back distant kinfolk like the news spreading that you got a job.

76. Say this Roosevelt is a fast worker. Even on Sunday when all a President is supposed to do is put on a silk hat and have his picture taken coming out of church, why this President closed all the banks, and called Congress in extra session. And that's not all he is going to call 'em if they don't get something done.

77. This fellow Roosevelt never gets through surprising us. We just find out now that he speaks French fluently. That's the second linguistic surprise he has handed us. The other was when the banks were closed. We knew he could speak English, but we dident know he could talk "American" till that night. In fact, he has three speaking accomplishments. He is the only guy who can talk turkey to the Senate.

78. Mr. Roosevelt stepped to the microphone last night and knocked another home run. His message was not only a great comfort to the people, but it pointed a lesson to all radio announcers and public speakers what to do with a big vocabulary—leave it at home in the dictionary. Some people spend a lifetime juggling with words, with not an idea in a carload.

79. Mr. Roosevelt made us a mighty fine speech over the radio Sunday night. He spoke our language. Not, "Bally-hoo the Nation to Prosperity"; "Nation in a tailspin"; "Can't make a Hit every time we come to Bat." And in addition to all this, he has the best radio voice in America.

Course he just read the minutes of the last meeting, but he did it so nice that we dident hardly notice that he forgot to mention what might be in his mind for the future.

80. I dont suppose there is any business with as many

unemployed as the "advising" business. What gets these big fellows' goat is Roosevelt listens to 'em all, but they cant tell whether he is paying any attention or not.

81. Yale gives President Roosevelt a degree. But they made him make a speech for it. Degrees are getting higher priced. That's the most anybody has given for one in years. The President kinder held up for his Brain Trust. He said he would take brains anytime in preference to politics. He just as good as admitted you couldent get both in the same body.

82. I wrote a little gag the other day about "appealing to the President for a guarantee," and I bet a lot of you thought it just to be writing. Well, get this in the papers today, "C. L. Bardo, President of the National Association of Manufacturers, asks the President the following:

"Business must have more definite ideas as to the direction in which the government is headed."

I can just see Mr. Roosevelt rushing in with a guarantee reading about as follows: "Nobody guaranteed me anything when I took over this job. No man gambles more than a President of the U.S. So you will pardon me if I am not able to guarantee business that it won't lose."

83. Everybody that is making money has it in for Roosevelt. You will have to explain that one yourself.

84. An awful lot of folks are predicting Roosevelt's downfall, not only predicting but praying. We are a funny people. We elect our Presidents, be they Republican or Democrat, then go home and start daring 'em to make good.

85. The one that I would stake my life on that Mr. Roosevelt has learned since he has been in there, is that people are willing to co-operate, but they are not going to willingly pay to do it. You can bet that his faith in human nature has had quite a jar.

86. This is dispatched just before the President goes on the air tonight. I am anxious to hear the comments in the Press. Even if its good there is plenty of 'em wont like it. He can speak on the Lord's Supper and he will get editorials against it. America is just like an insane asylum, there is not a soul in it will admit they are crazy. Roosevelt being the warden at the present time, us inmates know he is the one that's cuckoo.

Will Rogers *(left)* and a fellow-performer in the Zack Mulhall Wild West Show at the St. Louis Exposition, June 1904.

Will Rogers and Lucille Mulhall, daughter of Colonel Zack Mulhall. Will spent some time on the Mulhall Ranch in Indian Territory (now Oklahoma), perfecting his art of riding and roping.

Will Rogers with his fellow actors during his first days in vaudeville, 1905, probably at Keith's Union Square Theatre, New York, N.Y.

Will Rogers (*left*) in one of his earliest motion pictures, *Cupid the Cowpuncher* (1920), with Gwin "Big Boy" Williams.

Will Rogers during his vaudeville days, 1904-1909.

124

Will in the *Ziegfeld Follies of 1916.*

125

Will's parody of Rudolph Valentino (*right*) in Hal Roach's *Uncensored Movies*, 1923.

Will Rogers and Dorothy Stone in *Three Cheers*, 1928-1929, the musical comedy in which he carried on for Fred Stone after that actor was injured in an airplane accident. *Bruce Quisenberry*

Will Rogers parodying Ernest Torrance's performance in *The Covered Wagon* in one of the few pictures Will himself produced, *Two Wagons Both Covered*, 1923.

Will Rogers in one of his greatest roles, David Harum, in the Fox Film
motion picture of 1934.

Will Rogers *(far right)* in *The County Chairman*, a Fox Film of 1935.

Three great "western" stars: (*left to right*) Tom Mix, Will Rogers, William S. Hart.

Two of America's greatest humorists: Will Rogers (*left*) and Irvin S. Cobb, in whose "Judge Priest" stories Will starred in motion pictures.

Will Rogers and Irene Rich in *So This Is London,* 1930.

Will Rogers in his last motion picture, *Steamboat Round the Bend*, released in 1935 after his death.

~~6~~

EDUCATION

"I am practically world famous for my ignorance,"[1] announced Will Rogers. He liked to appear illiterate, for that tag suited his alter ego and gave him much larger scope for deflating the pompous, the smug and the sophisticated. Although he attended a number of schools in his early years, he did not distinguish himself as a scholar in any of them, a fact he often deplored.

"The fourth reader [McGuffey's] is as far as I ever got in schools," he wrote. "I am not braggin' on it. I am thoroughly ashamed of it for I had every opportunity."[2]

Will did have the best advantages the times afforded, and his parents were determined their son should have a good education, but getting him to embrace it was another matter.

Since there were no schools near the Rogers ranch, his mother taught him at home, but the active and determined lad, who cared only for a rope and a pony, did not have any time to devote to irksome book learning. When he was eight years old, his parents sent him to stay with his sister Sallie and her husband Tom McSpadden, so that he could attend his first school, Drumgoole, an Indian

[1] Weekly article, February 19, 1933.
[2] Weekly article, January 8, 1933.

134

school supported by taxes from the Cherokee Nation. Years later, he wrote of it:

> Drumgoul [*sic*] was a little one-room log cabin, four miles west of Chelsea. It was all Indians kids when there and I being part Cherokee had enough white in me to make my honesty questionable. There must have been about 30 of us in that room that had rode horseback and walked miles to get there. We graduated when we could print our full name and numerate to the teacher the Nationality of the last Democratic President.[3]

Apparently he must have been able to meet these requirements, for his father thought he had a better plan for him the following year. His sister May was attending Harrell Institute, a girls' school in Muskogee (Indian Territory), so their father made arrangements with its president to permit Will to go to school there and have his lessons with the President's son, Bob Brewer. They felt this experience would have a good influence on the boys. Will spent almost two years in this school for young ladies and did not leave an enviable record.

"I used to go to school here at a girl's school," he wrote after making a relief tour appearance in Muskogee in 1931. "That's a fact. Myself and the President's son were the only boys there. We even roomed in a great big dormatory with the girls. We were ten years old. I better quit before I get too far into this."[4]

After the death of his mother, Will attended a Presbyterian mission school in Tahlequah for one term. His next school was Willie Halsell College, in Vinita, where he

3 Weekly article, September 29, 1929.
4 Weekly article, February 22, 1931.

spent more than three years. He was happy there. Many of the leading families in that area sent their young people to Willie Halsell, where they studied music, elocution, the basic principles of arithmetic, English and history.

In the summer of 1895 Professor J. C. Shelton came into the Cherokee Nation seeking students for Scarrett College, and before he knew it, Will was at school in Neosho, Missouri. His love of roping and playing pranks were not in keeping with the serious curriculum laid down by the Methodist fathers of the institution, so he spent little more than a year there.

> By this time Clem Rogers was quite concerned about his son. He came to the conclusion that a more rigid form of training would be good for the young man, so he took him to Boonville, Missouri, and enrolled him in Kemper Military School, January 13, 1897.[5]

At first military life appealed to Will, for he was proud of his uniform with the brass buttons down the front. His grades fluctuated somewhat as his report card for March 26, 1897, shows: 100 in U.S. history; 65 in algebra; 65 in bookkeeping; and an average grade of 79. His demerits for the month were 50. He soon found that with all the restrictions placed on him he was accumulating more demerits than credits and much of his time was spent walking the "bull ring." He said in one of his articles:

> In 1898 Kemper Military School was not being run in accordance with the standards that I thought befitting a growing intellect. I was spending my third year in the fourth grade and wasn't

5 *Cadet Days of Will Rogers,* published by Kemper Military School, 1935.

being appreciated, so I not only left them flat during a dark night, but the entire school business for life.[6]

Unknown to his family, he ran away to Texas, where he found a warm welcome and good living on the Ewing ranch at Higgins, and spent some time there as a ranch hand.

Though Will's formal education ended with his sudden departure from Kemper, he had a basic foundation and was much better educated than many of the young men in the Cherokee Nation. The so-called colleges he attended were on a high school level, but they had splendid instruction and would compare favorably with the sophomore year in college in the present-day course of study. In all, he attended school for about ten years.

Will had an amazing memory; he could read anything once and remember it. He was quick to grasp things and did not have to spend long hours over his books. Besides, he preferred to have some fun. He had an inquiring mind that caused him to want to see things for himself and sent him on travels all over the world. His love of people and the exchange of ideas, coupled with his intense reading, made him one of the best informed men of his time.

His many uses of incorrect speech and grammar fitted his character of cowboy-philosopher. Of course, he knew better! When his friend Dr. James Whitcomb Brougher called to his attention that people criticized his syntax, he laughed and said, "Have they put a tax on sin? I am not surprised, as the Government is puting a tax on everything." Then the good minister told him it was his grammar with which the people found fault. Will replied, "Well, I just talk naturally and if there is any bad gram-

6 Weekly article, March 7, 1926.

mar, it ain't intentional. And I haven't heard that grammars are the best sellers."[7]

His disarming humor made him loved by all classes of people. To the underprivileged and uneducated he symbolized the triumph of the common man. The scholars, purists and educators realized he had an uncommon ability to discover truth and the courage to speak it, clothed in his own whimsical style. They were great admirers of Will Rogers.

At the height of his career several colleges wanted to confer degrees on him, but he always refused, as shown in his reply when Dr. Hamilton Holt, of Rollins College made the proposal: "Now what in the world would I be doing with a degree? A lot of guys that earned 'em dont know what to do with 'em, much less me that wouldent know what one was."[8]

He helped many young people through school by paying their expenses, and to make them feel better he always emphasized that he did not have an education.

If Will had spent more time in the class room in diligent study, conforming to the rules and regulations, the procedure might have stifled that rugged native power of his mind and restrained his effervescent wit. He just would not have been Will Rogers.

Education

1. Everybody is ignorant only on different subjects.

2. When ignorance gets started it knows no bounds.

[7] James Whitcomb Brougher, *Life and Laughter.*
[8] Weekly article, November 18, 1934.

3. Everybody has swimming pools but nobody has got a plain old geography. If a thing is particularly useless it gives you more credits. Most of our work is skilled and requires practice and not education. Like everything else you got to judge it by results. Here we are better educated (according to educational methods) than we ever were, and we are worse off than we ever were, so it's not living up to its billing.

4. An educated man just teaches the thing that he has been taught, and it's the same that everyone else has been taught that has read and studied the same books that he has.

5. When you walk up and ask for a job, you know you know your business, and no man out of a book knows if he knows his or not.

6. I believe the Lord split knowledge up among his subjects about equal after all. The so-called ignorant is happy. Maybe he is happy because he knows enough to be happy. The smart one knows he knows a lot, and that makes him unhappy because he cant impart it to all his friends. Discontent comes in proportion to knowledge. The more you know the more you realize you dont know.

7. There is nothing as stupid as an educated man if you get him off the thing he was educated in.

8. In [the old] days boys wanted an education whether they got a fraternity pin or not. They even had reading, writing and arithmetic, instead of football. Up to then boys had gone there for their heads and not their shoulders.

9. You cant beat education for foolishness. There has always been a problem "Does Education Pay?" Yes, it does, if you got a sense of humor. You got to pay for your laughs at a show, so why not at school?

10. The more you know, the more you think somebody owes you a living.

11. Education never helped morals. The most savage people we have are the most moral. The smarter the guy, the bigger the rascal.

12. Robbing is one profession that certainly has advanced in this country. No schools or anything to learn you to rob. No other line, outside of drinking can show the progress that robbing has in the last five years. We spend billions of dollars on education and we are no smarter today than thirty years ago, and we spend nothing to foster robbing, and here it is one of the most skilled industries we have. So it sometimes

140

makes you think whats the use of learning people anything anyway. Let 'em alone, and they will progress quicker.

13. You must never tell a thing. You must illustrate it. We learn through the eye and not the noggin.

14. They say children in kindergarten must play in order to get 'em to learn. What do you mean children? Cross word puzzles learned grown folks more words than school teachers. And what arithmetic the women folks know they got at a bridge table. Our splendid English comes from attending the movies. My geography comes from an airplane window. Yes sir, there is 120 million in the American Kindergarten.

15. If nations held 'em [intelligence tests] I dont believe we would be a favorite to win.

16. Naval training will drive millions of Americans to a geography.

17. It's open field running that gets your old college somewhere and not a pack of spectacled orators or a

mess of civil engineers. It's better to turn out one good coach than ten college Presidents. With College Presidents, as far as publicity is concerned, they just as well might have matriculated in Hong-Kong.

18. These baccalaureate addresses dont offer 'em much encouragement outside of advising 'em to vote the straight Republican ticket.

19. Villians are getting as thick as college degrees and sometimes on the same fellow.

20. Professors are just like actors. Actors got press agents that write things about them and they get so they believe it. Professors get to looking at their diploma and get to believing what it says there. And they forget they got that diploma on their *memory* and not on their sense.

21. *Will is offered an honorary degree.*

Degrees have lost prestige enough as it is without handing 'em around to second-hand comedians, and its this handing 'em out too promiscously that has helped to cheapen 'em. Let a guy get in there and battle four years if he wants one, and dont give him one just because he happens to hold a good job in Washington, or manufactures more monkey-wrenches than anybody else or because he might be fool enough to make people laugh.

Keep 'em for those kids that have worked hard for 'em. Keep 'em believing in 'em. They are stepping out in the world with nothing but that sheet of paper. That's all they got. Our civilization dont offer 'em anything else. We offer him nothing. He steps into a world not of his making, so lets at least dont belittle his badge.

22. Actual knowledge of the future was never lower, but hope was never higher. Confidence will beat predictions any time.

23. I think you can learn the same at all schools outside of football.

24. *Re* Smith College:

It's an awfully common name but a mighty nice college.

25. Harvard is the home of culture and poor football. Everyone in Harvard can speak good English but nobody can make a touchdown.

26. All of our disgustingly rich men are at a loss to know
    what to do with their money. Funny none of them
    ever thought of giving it back to the people they got
    it from. Instead of these men giving money to found
    colleges to promote learning, why dont they pass a
    constitutional ammendment prohibiting anybody from
    learning anything? And if it works as good as the
    Prohibition one did, in five years we would have the
    smartest race of people on earth.

27. That's one thing about history, it never has to explain
    anything. It just gives you the bare facts and there
    is no way of cross-examining them to find out.

28. History is all we got to go by and history dont record
    that economy ever won a war.

29. If every history or books on old things was thrown in
    the river and everybody had nothing to study but the
    future, we would be about 200 years ahead of what
    we are.

30. A lot of guys have had a lot of fun joking about
    [Henry] Ford because he admitted one time that he
    dident know history. He dont know it, but history will
    know him. He has made more history than his critics
    has ever read.

31. [Scientists] can tell you just to the minute when something is going to happen ten million miles away but none of them has ever been smart enough to tell you what day to put on your heavy underwear.

32. A scientist is a man that can find out anything and nobody in the world has any way proving whether he found it out or not, and the more things he can think of that nobody can find out about, the bigger scientist he is.

33. One thing about economics and money theories. Your theory is always right for its never been tried.

34. Some guy invented "Vitamin A" out of a carrot. I'll bet he cant invent a good meal out of one.

35. A man only learns by two things; one is reading and the other is association with smarter people.

36. People could read in [the old] days. They wanted to know what was going on, not what kind of a hat some guy had on. Your looks meant nothing to them. It was what you did that counted.

145

37. I dont envy the man that cant read because he certainly is not missing anything nowadays, and he is forming his own opinion without having someone else form it for him. The most real, down-to-earth horse sense men in America are the ones that cant read. I'll bet they are more right on any question than the so-called smart fellow.

38. More words aint good for anything in the world only to bring on more argument.

39. I got me a dictionary one time, but goodness it dident last long. It was like looking in the telephone book. I never called up anybody in my life if I had to look up their number. Nobody is worth looking through all those number for and thats the way it was with my dictionary. I could write the article while I was trying to see what the word meant, and thats one good thing about language, there is always a short word for it. Course, the Greeks have a word for it, and the dictionary has a word for it, but I believe in using your own for it.

40. Confucius prespired out more knowledge than the U.S. Senate has vocalized out in the last fifty years.

41. All this exchange of talk [in panel discussions] is a lot of hooey. It changes nobody or effects no opinions, but its kinder like weather-talk. It does no harm. But if one ever travels through your town, go hear it. It's the old cracker-barrel argument over again.

146

~ 7 ~

TRAVEL

Will loved to travel and absorbed a great deal on his trips because he was interested in everything he saw and everybody he met. Just keeping the date line on his daily telegram as he journeyed from city to city and country to country makes a surprising study in geography. As Mrs. Rogers often remarked, "Will was like a little boy that never grew up. He always wanted to go some place."

He was the greatest booster for aviation our country has ever had and did more than any other private citizen to promote air travel. Because he flew so much when the industry was in its primary stages, he gave confidence and approval to this then new mode of transportation.

Will felt it was essential in his work as a speaker and writer to get first hand information on world events. As he stated, "I crossed and uncrossed about all the oceans we got, but its always been because I wanted to get somewhere. It never was just really for relaxation and pleasure."[1]

Any kind of a trip was fun for Will; by rail, air, car, horse or carriage—just so he was traveling.

Will visited Russia several times, for the country always held deep interest for him. After his trip there in 1926 he wrote a book about it which he called *There's Not a*

[1] Weekly article, February 19, 1933.

Bathing Suit in Russia. Some of the things he said are strangely prophetic; other statements are as true today as the day they were written.

In 1934 Will took Mrs. Rogers and their two sons, Will, Jr., and Jimmie, on an extensive tour into Russia on their trip around the world. He shows a deep understanding of the country and the people in the articles he wrote as well as in the radio broadcasts he made after that trip.

He and Wiley Post had originally planned to fly on to Russia in 1935, but their tragic flight ended at Point Barrow, Alaska, on August 15.

Travel

1. Nothing thickens one like travel.

2. You dont know what a country we have got till you start prowling around it. Personally, I like the small places and sparsely populated states.

3. Never look at a town with one of its prominent citizens. You have just seen what he wants you to see. I always get me a taxi and go prowling.

4. Brigham Young originated mass production, but Henry Ford was the guy that improved on it. He

alone is absolutely responsible for this great era of transportation in which we half-way live.

5. If you want to have a good time, I dont care where you live, just load in your kids and take some congenial friends and start out. You would be surprised what there is to see in this great country within 200 miles of where any of us live. I dont care what state or town.

6. I have never yet seen a man in such a big hurry that a horse or train wouldent have got him there in plenty of time. In fact nine-tenths of the people would be better off if they had stayed where they are, instead of going where they are going. No man in America if he dident get where he is going would be missed. People nowadays are traveling faster, but they are not getting any further, in fact, not as far as our old Dad's did.

7. The present generation doesent know what a milestone is. They go by so fast nowadays that miles mean nothing.

8. Trouble with American transportation is that you get somewhere quicker than you can think of a reason

149

for going there. What we need now is a new excuse to go somewhere.

9. No wonder American people are filling roads, trains, and air. There is so much to see. What we lack in reading, we make up in looking.

10. America is never in a better humor or feeling better than when moving, so all this traveling (even if it's walking) is a mighty good omen.

11. America has been muscle bound from holding a steering wheel. The only callous place on an American is the bottom of his driving toe.

12. The trouble with America is they are not "running" minded, we are kinder "riding" minded.

13. The manufacturers say [in 1923] in ten years there will be an automobile to every man, woman and child in the U.S. Now all they got to do is control the birth rate.

14. They have the same cars every year, only painted different.

15. Our automobiles dont stay at home long enough to know where homes are even if they could get back.

16. One way to solve the traffic problem would be to keep all the cars that are not paid for off the streets. Children could use the streets for playgrounds then.

17. If we can keep the young happy and the old satisfied, all the middle-aged have to look out for is women automobile drivers.

Foreign Countries

18. If you have never written an autobiography, you havent signed a foreign hotel register.

19. No sir, Europe has nothing to recommend it but its old age, and the Petrified Forest in Arizona would make a sucker out of it for age. Why that forest was there and doing business before Nero took his first violin lesson.

20. [Belgium is] the Gettysburg of Europe. Its really not a Country, but a military highway.

151

21. Canada is a mighty good neighbor and a mighty good customer. That's a combination that is hard to beat.

22. *Re* Nice:

It's pronounced Neece. Not Nice. They have no word for nice in French.

23. Paris was built just to entertain.

24. Rome has more churches and less preaching in them than any city in the world. Everybody wants to see where St. Peter was buried, but nobody wants to try to live like him.

If you stole from the barbarians you were indexed in your history as a Christian.

I dident know before I got there and they told me all this—that Rome had Senators. Now I know why it declined.

25. When nations in those days had nothing else to do they would take Rome, then sit and pray for somebody to come and take it off their hands.

26. [Switzerland is] the rumor factory of the world. They have neither imports nor exports. It's sole commodities are Conferences and Neutrality.

27. There is nothing that irks a Turk so much as peace.

28. The thing that really makes any two nations a little more sympathic towards each other is the fact they may be able to use each other.

29. Naturally every nation wants to protect themselves according to their own needs.

30. Every nation in Europe goes to bed with a gun under its head.

31. When you have fought each other as much as they have this old trusting each other to never have another war is a lot of beautiful stuff but not what you would want to build our whole mode of defense on. They want peace, but they want a gun to help to get it. Nations are not there so much to protect their little gunboats as they are their national prestige.

32. All those nations over there have been hating each other for years and they cant hate us as bad as they hate each other. They have got it in for each other because every one of them owns land. There is not a piece of land in Europe that every nation over there aint owned it themselves at some particular time, and every one of them is going to try to get it back just as soon as the other bird is not looking.

33. These big babies aint going to give anybody any thing. That's why they are big.

34. A Nation is built on character the same as a person is and no matter what their financial difficulties are that Old Character shows up.

35. I think a country is harder to understand than a woman. It's heart is not at its capital as some think.

36. No Nation has a monopoly on good things. Each one has something that the others could well afford to adopt.

37. Russia is starving her own people to feed propaganda to the rest of the world.

38. Russia has been pretty quiet for the last couple of weeks. They are studying some devilment to pull on the rest of the world. A Russian just loves misery and he wants to get as many in on it as he can.

39. That is one thing about the Russian—he thrives on adversity. He is never as happy in his life as when he is miserable. So he may just be setting pretty, for he is certainly miserable. It may be just the land for a Comarade to want to hibernate in.

40. I have always claimed that that's why they [the Russians] was such great parachute jumpers, was because they was disappointed when it opened.

41. [Russian] marriage and divorce laws are patterned after Hollywood and Park Avenue. Only they eliminate the lawyer. So it gives the poor a chance to get a divorce that over here would only be obtainable by the rich.

42. To get any kind of idea of Russia, everything in the world we do, every viewpoint we have, every matter of fact of looking at anything is entirely different in Russia. I was surprised they dident walk on their hands instead of their feet, just to be different from capitalistic nations.

43. Now the main question everybody asks me is "Are they happy?" That's a tough one to answer. There are millions of people in Russia. I couldent talk their language, so I couldent ask them are you happy. It's awful hard to look at a person and tell just how happy they are. Some of you look awful curious to me. Now we looked at 'em for eight days at hundreds of stations, crossing the Trans-Siberian railway. We'd see the people come down to the trains and just stand there. They'd be standing at the station with a dull, blank expression on their faces—no joy, no smile. They just looked like they dident know what the future held in store for 'em. But I've sat in the gallery of the Senate, and in the gallery of the House of Representatives in Washington and I've seen the same dull, blank expression—not knowing what the next election held in store for 'em.

44. Then too, it's not just what you'd call a good year for happiness in any part of the world anyhow. It's what you might call an off year for happiness. And then too, here's what everybody tells me, the Russians are naturally a sad people. They dont feel good until something's really the matter with them. In other words, a Russian aint happy till he's hurt. He thrives on pain. So to answer the question, "Is Russia happy?" I should answer, "Yes." For they've certainly got enough the matter with 'em to make 'em happy.

45. Russians I dont think would ever be as happy as we

are anyhow, for they havent got as much to laugh at as we have here. Perhaps we're not the most humorous people in the world, but the provocations to humor is greater in this country than anywhere else in the world. There's not a minute that there's not some of us doing something seriously that brings smiles to everybody else over here.

46. It seems the whole idea of Communism, or whatever they want to call it, is based on propaganda and blood. Their whole life and thought is to convince somebody else. It looks to me like if a thing is so good and is working so grand for you, you would kind of want to keep it to yourself. I would be afraid to let anybody in on it, and that generally seems to be about the usual brand of human nature over here. But the Communist has so many good things he just wants you to join in and help him use some of them.

47. One thing that a Communist can do is explain. You can ask him any question in the world, and if you give him long enough he will explain their angle, and it will sound plausible then. Communism to me is one-third practice and two-thirds explanation.

48. A Conservative thinks you ought to divide with him what you have while a real Communist believes that you ought to give it all to him, in exchange you call

him Comrade. It's like Prohibition; it's a good idea but it wont work.

49. It just looks to me like Communism is such a happy family affair that not a communist wants to stay where it is practiced. It's the only thing they want you to have but keep none themselves.

50. The old Communist preaches his doctrines, but he wants to do it where he is enjoying the blessing of capitalistic surroundings. He preaches against the pie, but he sure eats it.

~ 8 ~

PHILOSOPHY AND RELIGION

"My humor is not so hot, my philosophy don't philo and my jokes are pre-war, but my good feeling toward mankind is 100 per cent,"[1] Will Rogers wrote to young Ed Sullivan, who was then a columnist on the New York *Daily News*. That perhaps characterizes the Rogers' philosophy better than anything else, for he could always find the good in people; beyond that, he did not bother.

To understand Will Rogers' deep respect for religion of any kind, his abiding faith in God and an almost Christlike gift of giving and trying to help others, we have only to go back to his forebears to know that these traits were inherent.

His parents, Mary America Schrimsher and Clem Vann Rogers, were descended from a distinguished line. While there was a trace of English and Welsh, it was the Irish and Cherokee Indian blood that predominated in their progeny.

Clem had settled in the Cherokee Nation near the Kansas line until the Civil War interrupted his mercantile and ranching activities. For four years he served the Confederacy under the gallant Indian leader, Brigadier General Stand Watie in the Cherokee Mounted Volunteers, and reached the rank of captain. On his return from

[1] Letter to Ed Sullivan, from the Unclassified Scrapbook, Will Rogers Memorial, 1932.

service, he had to work very hard to recover some of the fortune he had lost during that time. So it was not until 1875 that he selected the picturesque site for their future home near the Verdigris River, about twelve miles from the present town of Claremore, Oklahoma.

The large white house with a central hall and with fireplaces at each gabled end showed definitely the influence of Southern architecture. Native cedars lined the sandstone walk from the front gate to the white portico and made an imposing setting for the yard, which was always a profusion of color and beauty under the capable hands of Mary Rogers.

It was a home of good living and deep affection, of religious and social activity. It was in this home that William Penn Adair Rogers was born on November 4, 1879.

There were few hotels in the rolling country known as Cooweescoowee District—of which Clem was a judge— and the Rogers home was a favorite stopping place for officials of the Cherokee Nation en route to council at Tahlequah, the capital.

"We then had our own government," Will recalled years later, "and the name of Oklahoma was as foreign to us as toothpaste."[2]

Circuit riders made it a point to visit there often, not only because Clem provided well for his family, but also because his wife Mary was deeply religious and any man who carried the Word of God was always welcome. "The only men Papa ever refused meals and lodging were those whose horses had cockleburs in their tails," my own mother[3] told us.

Will's mother died when he was ten years old, and

3 Will's sister Sallie (Mrs. Thomas McSpadden).
2 Weekly article, September 29, 1929.

somehow he always carried the hurt of this parting. Instinctively his heart was touched by anyone who was motherless. His sisters, Sallie, Maud and May, were devoted to him and left nothing undone for their young brother. His father seldom denied him anything. To them he was always someone very special. Neighboring ranchers and all the relatives felt he belonged to them. Their homes were always open to "Uncle Clem's boy." It was this love he prized so much that he never grew apart from the "home folks." In fact, his years of success intensified his love for his people, and it was no wonder everyone in the Southwest claimed kin to him.

In his marriage he was extremely fortunate, for Betty Blake was the perfect companion for the restless trick roper she married in 1908. She was willing to troupe with him on the vaudeville circuit and make a home for him in a hotel room, just as she presided with gracious dignity in their California home when she never knew how many people he would bring to the dining table or ask others to visit indefinitely. She understood his nature perhaps better than anyone else and made him feel free to pursue the things he wanted to do. She helped him see his own potential gifts and skillfully aided in bringing them to fulfillment. Will relied on her judgment, leaving many important decisions up to her. He adored his children to the extent that he could never find it in his heart to correct them—a task he also left up to their mother.

Some of Will's best friends were preachers. They were unconsciously drawn to him and hung on the words he said. They realized he was not merely a wisecracking joker, for beneath his pertness of expression there was a depth of philosophy. Along with others, they knew he was a thinker and were well aware of his keen analysis of any situation.

161

"I hold the distinction of being the only one that ever preached a sermon in a regular church and dident know it," he wrote after he spoke to a congregation in Canton, Ohio, at the request of the minister, "and I dont even know what denomination the church was."[4]

After his first "lecture" appearance which was made in a church in Elmira, New York, he said, "In making this tremendous leap from the *Follies* to the pulpit, I did not have to change one word of my act. I dont know whether its a compliment to the church audience or the *Follies* audience."[5]

The Reverend James Whitcomb Brougher, a Baptist minister of Glendale, California, was one of his best friends—a very able, charming man and somewhat of a humorist himself. They held several debates on the subject, "*Resolved*, That Cowboys Have Been More Beneficial to Mankind Than Preachers."[6] This was an excellent type of performance as well as thought provoking. "He proved that talking and not preaching is appreciated,"[7] Will wrote. It was Dr. Brougher who spoke the words of consolation at Will's funeral in Forest Lawn Cemetery in 1935. "The greatest honor, yet the most diffcult service I ever conducted," he told us later.

The Rogerses were never a part of the smart Hollywood set of cafe society. They had a world of friends among all the different groups of California artists, but it was the simple, wholesome entertainment they sought. They tried to keep to themselves, but there was always a long line of relatives and friends about them.

"Above all, Rogers' life has been as clean as a whistle," said O. O. McIntyre. "He never wrote or spoke a dirty

4 Weekly article, October 18, 1925.
5 Ibid.
6 Weekly articles, December 16, 1923; April 13, 1924.
7 Weekly article, November 25, 1923.

line. There is not one tiny black mark against him."[8]

Will had a boyish enthusiasm for anything he undertook, no matter what it was—a trip, a game of polo, the World Series, a new play, helping his friends, roping calves or just talking. He had a deep sense of humility and never realized his own greatness in any line. He did not fret or brood over things that had happened. To him yesterday was gone and done with, but he lived every minute of today. "We are living in a great time. Something to get excited about every minute,"[9] he wrote less than two months before his death.

The complete story of Will Rogers, the humanitarian, will never be told for he seldom revealed what he did, and many who greatly benefited by his bounty were slow to admit it. He felt that he had been lucky and because of that tried to help everyone else who had not been so fortunate. It would be impossible to name even the outstanding things he did to help others, so only a few can be mentioned here.

In World War I, when his salary was a modest one, he gave the Red Cross $100 each week for the duration and sold countless Liberty Bonds. Sunday nights in New York always found him playing some benefit and often two or three the same night. "I don't think any actor of his generation played more benefits than he did; certainly no one played them with more grace and honest enthusiasm," his wife remarked.[10]

Nor were his activities confined to America. While he was in Europe in 1926 a London paper told this story: "Refusing a check that would have amounted to probably $16,000 or more is what Will Rogers did in England

8 *Tulsa* [Oklahoma] *World*, December 24, 1933 (McNaught Syndicate) (microfilm).
9 Daily telegram, July 4, 1935.
10 Betty Rogers, *His Wife's Story*.

163

last week, and that gracious act was after saving a show from a flop and recouping C. B. Cochran, the producer of the show, to the amount of $60,000 by appearing in the production."[11]

In September of that same year he flew to Dublin to give a benefit for the Drumcollogher Relief Fund, raising more than 2,000 pounds. Nicaraguans will never forget his coming to aid them with financial assistance and good cheer in 1931 after their terrible earthquake and fire. They were the first to issue commemorative stamps honoring him. He flew to New Orleans in 1927 to give a benefit for flood relief, and the city was not lacking in appreciation for the $49,195.68 he raised for them.

In 1931 he arranged a series of benefits for the drought-stricken areas in Texas, Oklahoma and Arkansas under the auspices of the Federation of Women's Clubs, saying, "When you get a group of women behind anything it is always a success." He raised over $300,000 for the cause, and in Tulsa alone made $29,504. This he did by taxing some of his rich oil friends who were in the audience. In each town he always gave something himself besides his services, and that gesture often cost him six performances a day.

Most people know about his taking Fred Stone's place in the musical comedy *Three Cheers* after Stone's airplane accident, but few know of the financial sacrifice he made to do it. One paper stated he canceled $500,000 in engagements to do this.[12] Some of the groups who had booked him had to be paid off for breach of contract, but on the whole most of the organizations were merely disappointed that they would not get to hear him and laugh with him. As Mr. Houston Hart of San Angelo,

11 *Ibid.*
12 Los Angeles *Examiner*, August 22, 1928.

Texas, wrote, "I wonder if Fred Stone really needs you half as much as we do?"[13] An American Legion Post in Texas asked $1,000 forfeit, and a wire from Will Rogers shows that he sent them $1,500. But friendship's love outweighed anything else, and in comparison the money meant nothing to Will Rogers.

He supported relatives, cowboys, actors and a varied assortment of friends. On tour he gave programs for the veterans, the crippled children, the hospitals, the jails and anyone who wanted him. He arranged with Helen Keller for several benefits for the blind, and among her wires is this touching one:

> I love you Will Rogers and I don't care who knows it. Your wonderful letter and contribution to the endowment fund for the Blind of America, I am trying so desperately to raise, have given me new courage. . . . Do not fear the scrutiny of the ten eyes in my fingers for they will certainly find the wild flowers of humor in your face.[14]

In 1933 he made a series of broadcasts for the Gulf Oil Company at a salary of $50,000, and he gave the entire amount to the Red Cross and the Salvation Army, the two organizations to which he consistently contributed. Evangeline Booth best describes his generous spirit in her wire to him:

> On behalf of our people toiling from sea to sea to alleviate suffering, and in the name of the hungry and destitute I send a heart of gratitude for your substantial sacrificial contribution. There are some

13 Letter, 1928, Memorial Files, Rogers Collection.
14 Telegram, May 21, 1930.

things in this world for which there are neither words nor rewards. This is one. I must leave it to the next. There a multitude in His name will call you blessed.[15]

Manners

1. Customs make manners. Manners are nothing more than common sense.

2. If a man is a gentleman he dont have to announce it. All he has to do is to act like one and let the world decide. No man should have to prove in court what he is or what he comes from.

3. When it comes to a showdown class will tell.

4. Breeding will tell even in a Democratic Convention.

5. If a town has any culture and tourists commence hitting it, your culture is gone. Tourists will rub it out of any town.

6. No one can tell you as much about it [high society] as the one who has just been on the edge.

15 Telegram, Chicago, June 21, 1933.

7. Emily Post tells everything [about opera] but how to enjoy the thing. The fellow that figures out how to enjoy opera in a foreign tongue without kidding himself or four-flushing has a fortune in store for him. . . . I found I was wrong on every line of the whole book. . . . I kept right on learning and from now on I am just mangy with etiquette.

Dress

8. More people should work for their dinner instead of dressing for it. Half the stiff bosom shirts worn nowadays, the laundry is due on them yet.

9. Mink and sable—that's the best financial barometer in the world.

10. Nothing makes people more alike than putting a dress suit on 'em.

11. Any Sunday could be made as popular [as Easter] at Church if you called 'em fashion shows.

Will never wore a dress suit, except in the movie As Young as You Feel. His formal costume was the blue serge suit that became a trade mark with him. He appeared at the most lavish parties, dinners and gatherings in his blue serge suit.

167

12. I stuck to the old Blue Serge with the mirror effect in the seat and knees. If it was good enough for Ponca City and Muskogee, it was good enough for Uncle Andy's temple of art [Carnegie Hall]. I was the only one that dident attempt to try to have on a dress suit.

13. I got the old Blue Serge double-breasted that has done such valliant service in pinches over in Europe, and my one piece shirt. In fact, I am the only one that ever went through Europe and never lost a shirt stud. She [Mrs. Rogers] had the suit brushed so much that I was afraid to sit down for fear I would slip off the seat.

14. I dident want a dress or Tuxedo, but I did want an old dark blue serge that I could get in the dining room on the boat with, so I found a little place open, not exactly second-hand, but they had been there so long they tasted like it. Then some black shoes, and a black tie, and I was ready to fool the head steward. I was just thinking some people plan for years to go to Europe and wonder what they will wear and all that hooey.

15. I was the only one who did not own a dress suit, so my clothes naturally was the only ones that did not smell of moth balls.

168

16. The gamest women can keep back tears in sorrow, they cant keep back in happiness.

17. If you let them have their way, you will generally get even with them in the end.

18. Some women are failures, just as well as men.

19. You cant pass a park without seeing a statue of some old Codgar on a horse, it must be his bravery, you can tell it isn't his horsemanship. Women are twice as brave as men, yet they never seem to have reached the statue stage.

20. There is nothing as determined as a woman that carries on, and there is millions of 'em.

21. Money and Women are the most sought after and the least known about of any two things we have.

22. In the old days a woman had to go out and practice

169

shooting for weeks, perhaps months before she would dare open up on the "better half." But with this marvelous invention, the automatic, the more hysterical she gets, and the more he dodges about, the more direct hits will be scored. If she had been compelled to use the old-time weapon the crime would never have happened, because the present day woman dont wear enough clothes to conceal a real six-gun. Women used to be the alleged "weaker sex" but the automatic and the sentimental jury have been the equalizer. Why divorce him when you can shoot him easier and cheaper?

23. If we can just improve their [women's] marksmanship, we can improve civilization. About every fourth fellow you meet nowadays ought to be shot.

24. If women must insist on having men's privileges they have to take men's chances.

25. The women, poor souls, havent added anything constructive to the art of politics. They take it too serious. I believe they would go further if they kinder ridiculed and kidded the men. They can do that in everything else, so why can't they in politics?

26. The first idea of giving [women] the vote was just

to use the vote. But the women contrary like they are, they wasent satisfied with that. They started to take this equality thing serious. They begin to think they really was somebody.

The women figured that "While we may not be as good as a man, we are at least as good as a politician." So the scamps commenced to want to get in on the loot. As soon as they found out a political job took no experience to hold, that it took only experience to get, why they commenced to making themselves rather embarrassing around the political employment bureau.

27. Of course, the Mother I know the most about is the Mother of our little group. She has been for 22 years trying to raise to maturity, four children, three by birth and one by marriage. While she hasent done a good job, the poor soul has done all that mortal human could do with the material she has had to work with.

28. The best way to get the low-down on women and daughters is to ask your wife.

Philosophy

29. You got to sorter give and take in this old world.

We can get mighty rich, but if we havent got any friends, we will find we are poorer than anybody.

30. Geography dont change human nature. If you are right, people are for you whether its in Africa or Siberia.

31. Rumor travels faster, but it dont stay put as long as truth.

32. Humanity is not yet ready for either real truth or real harmony.

33. What's the matter with the world? There aint nothing but one word wrong with everyone of us, and that's selfishness.

34. The best way to condemn a thing is to know something about it.

35. The best way to judge just how good a man is, is to find out how he stands around his home and among his kind of people.

36. That's all there is to success is satisfaction.

37. We may elevate ourselves but we should never reach so high that we would ever forget those who helped us get there.

38. Be sure you are right and then go ahead, but dont arbitrate.

39. I sometimes wonder if the Lord is going to make the proper distinction between the fellow that means well and' the one that does well. I dont believe He will blackball us just because we dont remember.

40. There is nothing as easy as denouncing. It dont take much to see that something is wrong, but it does take some eyesight to see what will put it right again.

41. No man is great if he thinks he is.

42. It's great to be great, but it's greater to be human.

43. A remark generally hurts in proportion to its truth.

44. The older we get the more "standpat" we get. The only change we want as we grow older is a change back to the things of our early life. We dont want a lot of new ones. Just because a thing is new dont mean that it is better.

45. Those were the great old days, but darn it, any old days are great old days. Even the tough ones, after they are over, you can look back on with great memories.

46. [There is] nothing like congenial friends to just sit around with nothing in particular to knock and a good word for all.

47. When there is no malice in your heart there can be none shown in your homes.

48. Everybody has got a scheme to get the world right again. I cant remember when it was ever right. There has been times when it was right for you and you and you, but never all at the same time. The whole thing is a teeter-board even when its supposed to be going good. You are going up and somebody is coming down. You cant make a dollar without taking it from somebody. So everytime you wish for

something for your own personal gain, you are wishing somebody else bad luck, so maybe that's why so few of our wishes come to anything.

49. I would rather be able to criticize a man than to apologize to him.

50. Happiness and contentment is progress. In fact that's all progress is.

Civilization

51. We will never have true civilization until we have learned to recognize the rights of others.

52. There aint no civilization where there aint no satisfaction and that's what's the trouble now. Nobody is satisfied.

53. If we see anything we want, we take it. The more so-called civilized we get the more we kill and take.

54. *When Will Durant asked Rogers to contribute to his "Living Philosophies," Rogers wrote:*

175

We are just here for a spell and pass on. Any man that thinks civilization has advanced is an egotist. . . . We know a lot of things we used to dident know, but we dont know any way to prevent 'em happening.

We have more tooth paste on the market and more misery in our courts than at any time in our existence. There aint nothing to life but satisfaction.

Indians and primitive races were the highest civilized because they were more satisfied and they depended less on each other and took less from each other. We couldent live a day without depending on everybody. So our civilization has given us no liberty or independence.

So get a few laughs and do the best you can. Take nothing serious for nothing is certainly depending on this generation. Each one lives in spite of the previous one and not because of it.

And dont start "seeking knowledge" for the more you seek the nearer the "booby hatch" you get.

And dont have an ideal to work for. That's like riding towards a mirage of a lake. When you get there, it aint there. Believe in something for another world, but dont be too set on what it is, and then you wont start out that life with a disappointment. Live your life so that whenever you lose you are ahead.

55. Politics is just a custom and has nothing whatsoever to do with civilization.

56. There is nothing that sets a nation back as far in civilization as prosperity.

57. The big [nations] would like to sorter stick together. They say its to protect the little ones, but its to protect themselves. There is no nation laying awake at night worrying about a little nation unless that little nation is one where somebody can march across to get to them. Brotherly love has never crossed a boundry line yet. Yes, sir, geography has more to do with brotherly love than civilization and Christianity combined.

58. I doubt very much if civilization (so called) has helped generosity. I bet the old cave man would divide his raw meat with you as quick as one of us will ask a down-and-out to go in and have a meal with us. Those old boys or girls would rip off a wolf skin breech clout and give you half of it quicker than a Ph.D would slip you his umbrella. Civilization hasent done much but make you wash your teeth, and in those days gnawing on bones and meat made tooth paste unnecessary.

59. Civilization has taught us to eat with a fork, but even now if nobody is around we use our fingers. Civilization is nothing but acquiring comforts for us.

60. That's one trouble with our charities, we are always saving somebody away off, when the fellow next to us aint eating. Something wrong with the Missionaries. They will save anybody if he is far enough away and dont speak our language. This is a time when I dont care where you live, you cant throw a rock without hitting somebody who needs help more than you do.

61. Any nation is a heathen that aint strong enough to punch you in the jaw. Between our Missionaries and our oil men we are just in wrong all over the world.

62. Missionaries are going to reform the world whether it wants it or not.

63. What degree of egotism is it that makes a nation or a religious organization think theirs is the very thing for China or the Zulus? Why, we cant even Christianize our legislators.

64. Now when they [Congress] get the Constitution all fixed up they are going to start in on the Ten Commandments, just as soon as they can find somebody in Washington who has read them.

65. The minute a thing is long and complicated it confuses. Whoever wrote the Ten Commandments made 'em short. They may not always be kept but they are understood. They are the same for all men.

Moses just went up on the mountain with a letter of credit and some instruction from the Lord and he just wrote 'em out and they applied to the steel men, the oil men, the bankers and the farmers and even the U.S. Chamber of Commerce.

I expect there is a lot of lessons in the Bible that we could learn and profit by and help us out, but we are just so busy doing nothing we havent got time to study 'em out. But in Moses time, the rich dident gang up on you and say, "You change that Commandment or we wont play."

66. You cant get far ridiculing a man for upholding the Bible, or even the dictionary if its his sincere belief.

67. That's one wonderful thing about the Bible. There was no censorship in those days. Of course now, some of our churches hold conferences and cut out certain parts they think dont belong in there, or change them to what they think should be said instead of what was said. In other words, we are always improving on the words of the Lord. That's even worse than a scenario writer brightening up Shakespeare.

179

68. Of course the Bible has always been "the best seller." But unless you are a real seeker of knowledge or of consolation, it sometimes gets hard to read for a dumb fellow, for there is so much that we cant understand. I dont suppose there is two preachers in the world that would absolutely interpret a whole chapter exactly alike, but any interpretation you put on it is good.

Death

69. Nobody wants to know who was born, but everybody is anxious to know who dies, and the better known they are the more anxious they are to read about their deaths.

70. Why is it the good ones are the ones that go? That's one thing about an onery guy, you never hear of him dying. He is into everything else but a coffin.

71. It's only the inspiration of those who die that makes those who live realize what constitutes a useful life.

72. Some honor to be killed by an earthquake. There is a certain amount of dignity to be preserved even in death.

73. You must judge a man's greatness by how much he will be missed.

74. What constitutes a life well spent? Love and admiration from our fellow men is all that anyone can ask.

75. Death knows no demonination; Death draws no color line. If you live right, Death is a joke to you as far as fear is concerned.

76. Us ignorant laugh at Spiritualists but when they die they go mighty peaceful and happy. After all, all there is to living is to go away satisfied.

77. Of course, we are all just hanging on here as long as we can. I dont know why we hate to go, we know it's better there. Maybe it's because we havent done anything that will live after we are gone.

78. *After his gall bladder operation in 1927, Will said:*

People couldent have been nicer to me if I had died.

79. When I die, my epitaph or whatever you call those

181

signs on gravestones is going to read: "I joked about every prominent man of my time, but I never met a man I dident like." I am so proud of that I can hardly wait to die so it can be carved. And when you come to my grave you will find me sitting there, proudly reading it.*

80. Well, anyhow, we are living in a great time. A fellow cant afford to die now with all this excitement going on.

Religion

81. They were very religious people that come over here from the old country. They were very human. They would shoot a couple of Indians on their way to every Prayer-meeting.

82. I was raised predominantly a Methodist, but I have traveled so much, mixed with so many people in all parts of the world, I dont know just what I am. I know I have never been a non-believer. But I can honestly tell you that I dont think that any *one* religion is *the* religion.

---

* One of his most famous and quoted remarks. First printed in the *Boston Globe*, June 16, 1930, after he had attended Tremont Temple Baptist Church, where Dr. James W. Brougher was minister. He asked Will to say a few words after the sermon. The papers were quick to pick up the remark, and it stayed with him the rest of his life. He also said it on various other occasions.

If I am broad minded in any way (and I hope I am in many) . . . I am broad-minded in a religious way. Which way you serve your God will never get one word of argument or condemnation out of me. There has been times when I wished there had been as much real religion among some of our creeds as there has been vanity, but that's not in any way a criticism.

83. It's mighty hard for a country or a duly accredited representative of a country to tell or even advise another country how to conduct their religious affairs. That's about the toughest business we got in any man's country to be monkeying with, is religion. It's the one thing, no matter be he Professor, or heathen, they think they have a right to do with it as they see fit, as long as they dont bother with anyone else.

84. These big wars over commerce, they kill more people but one over religion is really the most bitter.

85. There is on argument in the world that carries the hatred that a religious belief does. The more learned a man is the less consideration he has for another man's belief.

86. I have worked at affairs for every denomination in

the world here in New York, because one is just as worthy as the other. Old New York, the so-called heartless city, houses some great people in every denomination in the world, and I cant see any difference in them. I havent been able to see where one has the monopoly on the right course to Heaven.

87. Can you imagine our Savior dying for all of us, yet we have to argue over just whether he dident die for us personally and not for you. Sometimes you wonder if His lessons of sacrifice and devotion was pretty near lost on a lot of us.

88. If some of these birds would follow His example instead of trying to figure out His mode of arrival and departure, they would come nearer getting confidence in their church.

89. If the Lord had wanted us to know exactly how and where we come from he would have let us know in the first place. He dident leave any room for doubt when he told you how you should act when you got here. His example, and the Commandments are plain enough, so just start from there. Never mind going back any farther.

The Lord put all these millions of people over the earth. They dont all agree on how they got here and

90% dont care. But He was pretty wise when He did see to it that they all do agree on one thing (whether Christian, Heathen or Mohammed) and that is the better lives you live the better you will finish. No great religious revival will ever be started from an argument over where we come from. The religious revival of the future, when it comes, if started, will be people's fear over where they are going.

90. It's better to let people die ignorant and poor believing in what they have always believed in, than to die prosperous and smart, half-believing in something new and doubtful.

91. There never was a nation founded and maintained without some kind of belief in something. Nobody knows what the outcome in Russia will be or how long this government will last. But if they do get by for quite a while on everything else, they picked the only one thing I know of to suppress that is absolutely necessary to run a country on, and that is religion. Never mind what kind, but it's got to be something or you will fail at the finish.

92. [For a man] to be allowed to have his spiritual guidance is not an unjust wage to demand for his toil.

93. The trouble with our praying is we just do it as a means of last resort. We just pray for a thing whether we got any dope on it or not.

94. If they are going to argue religion in the church instead of preaching it, no wonder you can see more people at a circus than a church.

95. Any old preacher that is having a time drafting anybody to listen to him, he announces that his sermon next Sunday night will be on "Hell and Damnation," or "I Am Going To Skin the Devil Alive and Show Up Hell." . . . He knew that title would catch 'em. He was looking for something sensational, and that's where the movies got the idea. Both of 'em out to be made to cut it out. A picture that cant draw without "Hell" in the title aint much picture, and a preacher than cant preach without "Hell" in his title is just as weak as the movies.

96. Preaching is one of the few things that folks have never been able to dope out exactly what its worth anyhow. Some preachers ought to pay admission to get into the church themselves, but as a rule preachers do a mighty good job and are underpaid.

Will Rogers and his aunt-by-marriage, Juliette Schrimsher. *International News Photo*

Will Rogers, citizen of the world,
goodwill ambassador.

Will on the driveway of his
Beverly Hills, California, home,
1927.

One of Will Rogers' last photographs, 1935. *Wide World Photos*

This heroic bronze statue of Will Rogers, by sculptor Jo Davidson, stands in the foyer of the Will Rogers Memorial, Claremore, Oklahoma. A second statue, cast from the same mold, is in Statuary Hall, Washington, D.C.

The Will Rogers Memorial, Claremore, Oklahoma. The tomb is at the lower far right.

Rogers' tomb, Claremore, Oklahoma. Here lie Will, his wife Betty, his infant son Fred.

~9~

MISCELLANEOUS

1. Art aint put-on when you are paying for it out of your own pocket.

2. [Ancestors] dont mean a thing in our tribe. It's as unreliable as a political promise. They no more take after their father and mother than a Congressman will take after a good example.

3. The Camera has made more criminals than bad environment.

4. It's getting so Christmas kills more people than it makes happy.

5. *Re* Congressional Record, mailed free:

Men are gradually realizing that a thing that is free

192

is of no earthly importance. It lost men more votes than it ever gained for them.

6. *Re* dial telephones:

You have to cuss yourself instead of some innocent girl.

7. [Divorce] aint so bad I guess when it's only the participants suffer, but it's sure tough on the children. Well, anyhow it's a great industry, and I guess about the only way to stop it is to stop marriage.

8. No man can be condemned for owning a dog. As long as he has a dog he has a friend and the poorer he gets the better friend he has.

9. Heroing is one of the shortest-lifed professions there is.

10. This thing of being a hero, about the main thing to it is to know when to die. Prolonged life has ruined more men than it ever made.

193

11. Heroes are made every little while, but only one in a million conduct themselves afterwards so that it makes us proud that we honored them at the time.

12. There aint nothing that breaks up homes, countries and nations like somebody publishing their memoirs.

13. I dont know opera but I know common sense and the commoner the better I know it.

14. Oblivion is a one-way ticket town.

15. Popularity is the easiest thing in the world to gain and it is the hardest thing to hold.

16. This is an age of progress. Live fast and die quick. The human side of anything cant compare with so-called progress.

17. Don't miss . . . Boulder Dam. It's the biggest thing that's ever been done with water since Noah made the flood look foolish.

18. There are two things I dont care how smart you are, you will never understand. One is an alienist's testimony and the other is a railroad timetable.

19. Retroactive, means as you were before you got like you are.

20. Like all things you leave to relatives, they get rid of them. You are better off if you leave 'em to outsiders.

21. The Lord so constituted everybody that no matter what color you are you require about the same amount of nourishment.

22. The man with a message is a whole lot harder to listen to.

23. I wonder if it aint just cowardice instead of generosity that makes us give most of our tips.

24. It's always a bird that never does anything that enjoys a vacation. There's nothing in the world as hard as playing when you dont want to.

25. A man should never take a vacation when he don't want one. You can't learn anything the first time, I don't care how smart you are. It takes years to learn how to vacate properly.

REFERENCES

REFERENCES

The following abbreviations are used throughout this list of references:

Bathing Suit—There's Not a Bathing Suit in Russia, 1927
Conv. article—From newspaper articles written at the political conventions
D.T.—Daily telegram
Letters—Letters of a Self-Made Diplomat to His President, 1926
More Letters—More Letters of a Self-Made Diplomat to His President, 1928
W.A.—Weekly newspaper article

CHAPTER 1

The Country

1. Speech at luncheon for Post and Gatty, Tulsa, Oklahoma, *Tulsa World*, July 14, 1931
2. W.A., October 10, 1926
3. W.A., November 30, 1930
4. W.A., May 4, 1924
5. W.A., April 17, 1932
6. *Letters*, 1926

7. W.A., March 22, 1931
8. W.A., May 3, 1931
9. W.A., December 28, 1924
10. W.A., October 5, 1924
11. W.A., September 3, 1933
12. W.A., December 6, 1925
13. *Letters,* 1926
14. W.A., November 13, 1927
15. W.A., October 19, 1930
16. W.A., June 1, 1930
17. W.A., March 12, 1933

The People

18. Squibbs radio talk, May 4, 1930
19. W.A., February 24, 1924
20. W.A., March 2, 1924
21. W.A., June 21, 1925
22. W.A., May 31, 1925
23. *Bathing Suit,* 1927
24. D.T., October 27, 1929
25. D.T., March 16, 1932
26. D.T., July 25, 1935
27. *Letters,* 1926
28. D.T., June 19, 1935
29. W.A., August 4, 1929
30. D.T., October 18, 1933
31. W.A., April 6, 1924
32. W.A., June 15, 1924
33. W.A., June 30, 1929
34. W.A., September 10, 1933
35. D.T., October 21, 1926
36. W.A., February 4, 1923

37. W.A., August 30, 1925
38. W.A., February 22, 1925
39. *Letters,* 1926
40. *Letters,* 1926
41. W.A., July 23, 1933
42. W.A., May 31, 1925
43. W.A., July 9, 1933

The U.S. Government

44. W.A., November 16, 1930
45. *Bathing Suit,* 1927
46. W.A., June 8, 1924
47. W.A., December 14, 1924
48. W.A., November 2, 1924
49. W.A., December 20, 1925
50. W.A., July 21, 1935
51. W.A., November 25, 1934
52. W.A., February 3, 1929
53. W.A., March 27, 1932
54. W.A., June 5, 1932
55. W.A., November 11, 1928
56. W.A., April 17, 1932
57. D.T., February 12, 1932
58. D.T., July 1, 1934
59. W.A., December 26, 1926
60. W.A., October 30, 1932
61. W.A., December 18, 1932
62. W.A., July 22, 1923
63. W.A., December 7, 1930
64. D.T., July 5, 1935
65. W.A., December 18, 1932

66. D.T., September 30, 1934
67. *Bathing Suit*, 1927

CHAPTER 2

Politicians

1. W.A., April 12, 1925
2. W.A., October 14, 1932
3. W.A., June 8, 1924
4. W.A., September 13, 1925
5. W.A., September 27, 1925
6. W.A., March 22, 1925
7. D.T., March 1, 1935
8. W.A., September 12, 1926
9. W.A., January 13, 1924
10. D.T., June 11, 1935
11. W.A., July 1, 1928
12. W.A., December 30, 1923
13. W.A., November 16, 1924
14. W.A., June 28, 1931
15. W.A., April 22, 1928
16. W.A., September 26, 1926
17. W.A., November 4, 1928
18. "A Letter to the *Times*," *Los Angeles Times*, November 10, 1932
19. W.A., October 19, 1924
20. W.A., October 19, 1924
21. W.A., November 16, 1924
22. D.T., September 10, 1934
23. W.A., September 12, 1926
24. W.A., July 15, 1923
25. W.A., September 16, 1928
26. W.A., October 4, 1925

27. W.A., January 1, 1933
28. W.A., November 11, 1928
29. D.T., March 16, 1934
30. D.T., June 5, 1929
31. D.T., November 18, 1934
32. W.A., February 3, 1929
33. D.T., July 14, 1933
34. W.A., November 11, 1928
35. W.A., August 25, 1929
36. W.A., April 22, 1928
37. W.A., March 29, 1925
38. W.A., January 17, 1932
39. W.A., November 27, 1932
40. W.A., November 11, 1928

Democrats

41. W.A., September 29, 1929
42. W.A., August 1, 1925
43. Conv. articles, Democratic Convention, June 20, 1932
44. W.A., October 28, 1928
45. Conv. articles, Democratic Convention, June 24, 1928
46. W.A., April 14, 1929

Republicans

47. W.A., September 27, 1931
48. D.T., November 8, 1934
49. D.T., November 2, 1934
50. W.A., August 17, 1930
51. Squibbs radio talk, May 25, 1930
52. W.A., September 30, 1928
53. W.A., September 14, 1930

54. W.A., October 19, 1924
55. W.A., February 10, 1929

Elections

56. W.A., December 27, 1931
57. W.A., May 10, 1925
58. "A Letter to the *Times*," *Los Angeles Times*, November 10, 1932
59. W.A., November 9, 1924

United States Senate and Senators

60. W.A., January 6, 1929
61. W.A., May 6, 1923
62. D.T., February 28, 1935
63. Conv. articles, Democratic Convention, June 23, 1924
64. D.T., March 6, 1935
65. "The Worst Story I've Heard Today," September 7, 1925
66. W.A., August 4, 1929
67. W.A., March 22, 1925
68. W.A., April 13, 1930
69. W.A., March 15, 1931
70. *More Letters*, 1928
71. W.A., May 17, 1925
72. W.A., October 21, 1923
73. D.T., July 5, 1933
74. W.A., September 8, 1929
75. W.A., March 20, 1927
76. *Letters*, 1926
77. W.A., June 30, 1929

CHAPTER 3

Business

1. W.A., April 7, 1929
2. W.A., May 18, 1924
3. W.A., March 23, 1930
4. W.A., July 15, 1923
5. W.A., September 29, 1929
6. W.A., December 28, 1924
7. W.A., March 12, 1933
8. W.A., March 22, 1925
9. W.A., April 12, 1925
10. W.A., January 3, 1926
11. D.T., March 1, 1931
12. W.A., April 10, 1932
13. W.A., August 24, 1930
14. W.A., October 14, 1923
15. W.A., November 30, 1924
16. D.T., May 14, 1935
17. W.A., October 30, 1927
18. W.A., March 12, 1933
19. W.A., July 23, 1933
20. W.A., December 30, 1934
21. W.A., November 27, 1932
22. W.A., November 10, 1929
23. W.A., December 1, 1929
24. W.A., April 13, 1930
25. W.A., February 24, 1929
26. W.A., June 15, 1924
27. Squibbs radio talk, May 4, 1930
28. W.A., May 6, 1923
29. W.A., May 1, 1933

30. W.A., July 28, 1935
31. W.A., July 28, 1935
32. W.A., April 22, 1928
33. W.A., December 2, 1923
34. W.A., November 11, 1923
35. D.T., March 16, 1927
36. W.A., January 14, 1923
37. W.A., January 14, 1923
38. D.T., December 30, 1934
39. W.A., May 3, 1925
40. W.A., November 20, 1927
41. W.A., July 28, 1935
42. W.A., March 2, 1924
43. D.T., June 15, 1931
44. D.T., February 4, 1935
45. D.T., February 19, 1935
46. W.A., July 28, 1935
47. W.A., August 11, 1935
48. D.T., July 16, 1935
49. W.A., May 31, 1925
50. W.A., May 31, 1925
51. W.A., May 31, 1925

CHAPTER 4

Bankers

1. W.A., March 9, 1924
2. W.A., March 18, 1923
3. W.A., July 24, 1927
4. Squibbs radio talk, May 4, 1930
5. D.T., October 11, 1929

6. W.A., July 6, 1930
7. W.A., March 19, 1933
8. W.A., February 6, 1927
9. W.A., October 25, 1931
10. W.A., April 3, 1932
11. W.A., June 4, 1933
12. W.A., August 11, 1935

Taxes

13. W.A., December 28, 1924
14. W.A., May 19, 1929
15. D.T., February 12, 1932
16. W.A., July 8, 1923
17. W.A., October 19, 1924
18. W.A., November 25, 1934
19. D.T., February 29, 1932
20. W.A., November 11, 1928
21. D.T., February 5, 1935
22. W.A., January 10, 1926
23. W.A., August 9, 1925
24. W.A., November 2, 1924
25. D.T., March 20, 1932
26. D.T., March 15, 1929
27. D.T., March 23, 1932
28. W.A., February 28, 1926
29. W.A., January 6, 1924
30. W.A., April 12, 1925
31. *Letters,* 1926
32. *Letters,* 1926
33. Gulf radio talk, April 7, 1935
34. W.A., February 17, 1935
35. W.A., November 2, 1924
36. W.A., August 11, 1935

CHAPTER 5

Presidents in General

1. D.T., October 22, 1933
2. W.A., March 8, 1931
3. W.A., March 24, 1929
4. W.A., July 8, 1928
5. W.A., October 4, 1931
6. W.A., November 20, 1932
7. W.A., July 1, 1928
8. W.A., July 10, 1932
9. Conv. articles, Republican Convention, June 16, 1932
10. W.A., December 14, 1930
11. D.T., November 1, 1929
12. W.A., May 29, 1932
13. W.A., August 21, 1932
14. W.A., September 22, 1929
15. W.A., October 23, 1932
16. W.A., November 6, 1932

George Washington

17. W.A., April 28, 1929
18. W.A., December 23, 1928
19. W.A., February 13, 1927
20. Squibbs radio talk, June 1, 1930
21. W.A., February 10, 1929
22. W.A., September 22, 1929
23. W.A., February 10, 1929
24. W.A., October 19, 1924
25. W.A., May 19, 1929
26. W.A., March 16, 1930
27. W.A., February 24, 1929

Thomas Jefferson

28. W.A., September 29, 1929
29. W.A., May 23, 1928
30. W.A., February 13, 1927
31. W.A., March 8, 1925

Andrew Jackson

32. W.A., December 18, 1927
33. W.A., October 16, 1927
34. W.A., February 5, 1928
35. W.A., February 5, 1928
36. W.A., July 15, 1928
37. W.A., July 19, 1925

Abraham Lincoln

38. W.A., Demember 23, 1928
39. W.A., October 19, 1924
40. W.A., May 16, 1926
41. W.A., December 26, 1926
42. W.A., June 28, 1931
43. W.A., Febrary 26, 1933
44. W.A., July 6, 1924
45. W.A., February 22, 1925
46. Squibbs radio talk, June 1, 1930
47. D.T., February 12, 1934
48. W.A., June 10, 1923
49. W.A., May 31, 1927
50. W.A., February 26, 1933

Theodore Roosevelt

51. W.A., July 19, 1931
52. W.A., August 9, 1925

53. W.A., February 22, 1925
54. W.A., November 11, 1923

William Howard Taft

55. W.A., June 10, 1923
56. D.T., February 28, 1930

Calvin Coolidge

57. W.A., December 2, 1923
58. W.A., November 16, 1924
59. Conv. articles, Democratic Convention, July 4, 1924
60. W.A., December 31, 1922
61. W.A., September 12, 1926
62. W.A., August 7, 1927
63. W.A., March 3, 1928
64. W.A., February 17, 1929
65. W.A., March 24, 1929

Herbert Clark Hoover

66. Squibbs radio talk, April 20, 1930
67. W.A., February 12, 1928
68. D.T., August 9, 1929
69. W.A., March 24, 1929
70. W.A., December 14, 1930
71. Squibbs radio talk, April 20, 1930
72. W.A., May 31, 1931
73. W.A., November 27, 1932

Franklin Delano Roosevelt

74. W.A., May 22, 1932
75. D.T., January 25, 1933

76. D.T., March 6, 1933
77. D.T., March 31, 1933
78. D.T., March 13, 1933
79. D.T., May 8, 1933
80. D.T., May 23, 1934
81. D.T., June 21, 1934
82. D.T., November 27, 1934
83. D.T., April 2, 1935
84. D.T., April 1, 1935
85. D.T., March 18, 1935
86. D.T., April 28, 1935

CHAPTER 6

Education

1. W.A., August 31, 1924
2. *Letters*, 1926
3. W.A., July 31, 1931
4. W.A., July 5, 1931
5. W.A., September 2, 1934
6. W.A., May 11, 1930
7. W.A., July 5, 1931
8. W.A., August 26, 1928
9. W.A., February 21, 1932
10. D.T., September 4, 1931
11. W.A., January 6, 1929
12. W.A., April 25, 1926
13. W.A., June 25, 1933
14. D.T., April 22, 1935
15. D.T., June 25, 1935
16. D.T., May 9, 1935
17. W.A., September 29, 1929
18. D.T., June 3, 1935

19. W.A., September 11, 1932
20. Newspaper Clipping (a New York paper) of a radio broadcast, January 27, 1935
21. W.A., May 19, 1935
22. D.T., September 19, 1933
23. W.A., May 16, 1926
24. W.A., March 3, 1929
25. Squibbs radio talk, June 15, 1930
26. W.A., January 4, 1925
27. W.A., July 12, 1925
28. W.A., January 16, 1927
29. W.A., January 13, 1929
30. Squibbs radio talk, June 1, 1930
31. W.A., February 1, 1925
32. W.A., January 13, 1929
33. W.A., October 15, 1933
34. D.T., September 19, 1932
35. W.A., October 4, 1925
36. W.A., December 21, 1924
37. W.A., July 26, 1925
38. *Bathing Suit,* 1927
39. W.A., October 29, 1933
40. W.A., July 5, 1931
41. W.A., March 5, 1933

CHAPTER 7

Travel

1. D.T., May 7, 1927
2. W.A., April 3, 1927
3. W.A., January 17, 1926
4. Squibbs radio talk, June 1, 1930
5. W.A., September 7, 1930

6. W.A., November 1, 1925
7. W.A., May 18, 1924
8. D.T., March 12, 1934
9. D.T., July 28, 1935
10. D.T., July 16, 1934
11. D.A., October 25, 1931
12. W.A., July 24, 1932
13. W.A., January 14, 1923
14. W.A., January 18, 1925
15. W.A., September 11, 1932
16. Interview, *Birmingham Post,* November 4, 1925
17. D.T., June 27, 1935

Foreign Countries

18. W.A., July 25, 1926
19. *Letters,* 1926
20. W.A., September 13, 1925
21. W.A., August 28, 1932
22. *Letters,* 1926
23. W.A., July 24, 1927
24. *Letters,* 1926
25. W.A., June 2, 1929
26. W.A., July 11, 1926
27. W.A., December 19, 1930
28. W.A., August 16, 1925
29. W.A., January 12, 1930
30. *Bathing Suit,* 1927
31. W.A., February 9, 1930
32. Squibbs radio talk, April 6, 1930
33. W.A., November 8, 1931
34. W.A., September 20, 1931
35. W.A., December 28, 1930
36. W.A., November 30, 1930

37. D.T., October 16, 1930
38. W.A., December 28, 1930
39. *Bathing Suit*, 1927
40. W.A., June 30, 1935
41. Gulf radio talk, October 7, 1934
42. Gulf radio talk, October 14, 1934
43. Gulf radio talk, October 14, 1934
44. Gulf radio talk, October 14, 1934
45. Gulf radio talk, October 14, 1934
46. *Bathing Suit*, 1927
47. *Bathing Suit*, 1927
48. W.A., November 6, 1927
49. *Bathing Suit*, 1927
50. W.A., January 11, 1931

CHAPTER 8

Manners

1. W.A., August 31, 1924
2. W.A., July 19, 1925
3. W.A., February 25, 1923
4. W.A., July 27, 1924
5. *Letters*, 1926
6. W.A., December 16, 1923
7. W.A., September 9, 1923

Dress

8. W.A., February 25, 1923
9. W.A., November 23, 1924
10. D.T., February 3, 1935
11. D.T., April 22, 1935
12. W.A., May 9, 1926

13. W.A., January 2, 1927
14. W.A., January 26, 1930
15. W.A., May 18, 1924

Women

16. W.A., July 27, 1924
17. W.A., February 7, 1926
18. W.A., April 3, 1927
19. D.T., April 2, 1934
20. W.A., June 9, 1935
21. W.A., May 20, 1934
22. W.A., September 20, 1925
23. W.A., April 18, 1926
24. W.A., November 1, 1925
25. W.A., July 8, 1928
26. W.A., March 31, 1929
27. Squibbs radio talk, May 11, 1930
28. W.A., October 24, 1926

Philosophy

29. W.A., June 1, 1930
30. W.A., August 17, 1924
31. W.A., March 9, 1924
32. W.A., July 15, 1923
33. D.T., March 10, 1935
34. W.A., January 1, 1928
35. W.A., November 21, 1926
36. W.A., July 29, 1928
37. Speech on Scribner, January 14, 1925
38. D.T., January 24, 1927
39. W.A., April 14, 1935
40. W.A., July 28, 1935

41. D.T., March 1, 1929
42. D.T., February 28, 1930
43. D.T., March 31, 1925
44. W.A., September 11, 1932
45. W.A., June 2, 1935
46. W.A., August 4, 1935
47. D.T., January 13, 1928
48. W.A., October 2, 1932
49. W.A., March 18, 1923
50. W.A., April 10, 1927

Civilization
51. W.A., November 18, 1923
52. W.A., January 5, 1930
53. W.A., March 16, 1930
54. W.A., July 5, 1931
55. W.A., September 4, 1932
56. D.T., April 2, 1933
57. W.A., July 7, 1935
58. W.A., January 20, 1935
59. W.A., January 20, 1935

Missionaries
60. D.T., March 22, 1932
61. W.A., February 6, 1927
62. W.A., November 8, 1924
63. W.A., April 10, 1927

The Bible
64. W.A., December 31, 1922
65. W.A., March 17, 1935

66. W.A., August 9, 1925
67. W.A., June 22, 1930
68. W.A., March 18, 1934

Death

69. W.A., January 30, 1927
70. W.A., October 25, 1931
71. D.T., March 7, 1933
72. W.A., July 12, 1925
73. W.A., August 9, 1925
74. W.A., August 9, 1925
75. W.A., May 24, 1925
76. D.T., July 7, 1930
77. Introduction to Charles M. Russell's *Trials Plowed Under*, 1926
78. Chapter XVI, *Our Will*, Scott Cunningham newspaper story, 1935
79. *Boston Globe*, June 16, 1930
80. W.A., June 30, 1935

Religion

81. W.A., June 10, 1934
82. W.A., January 8, 1933
83. W.A., January 15, 1928
84. W.A., September 8, 1929
85. W.A., January 20, 1924
86. W.A., May 24, 1925
87. W.A., April 7, 1935
88. W.A., January 20, 1924
89. W.A., July 19, 1925
90. *Bathing Suit*, 1927
91. *Bathing Suit*, 1927

92. W.A., January 15, 1928
93. W.A., May 11, 1930
94. W.A., January 20, 1924
95. W.A., September 11, 1932
96. W.A., January 8, 1933

CHAPTER 9

1. W.A., April 5, 1931
2. W.A., August 4, 1929
3. D.T., December 30, 1927
4. W.A., December 28, 1924
5. W.A., April 27, 1924
6. D.T., March 25, 1935
7. W.A., September 21, 1930
8. W.A., May 8, 1927
9. W.A., February 15, 1925
10. D.T., July 17, 1928
11. W.A., March 20, 1932
12. W.A., December 23, 1934
13. W.A., October 24, 1926
14. W.A., February 5, 1933
15. Squibbs radio talk, May 5, 1930
16. W.A., April 4, 1926
17. D.T., September 6, 1932
18. W.A., August 24, 1925
19. W.A., July 15, 1934
20. W.A., February 13, 1927
21. W.A., May 8, 1927
22. W.A., June 24, 1923
23. W.A., November 25, 1923
24. W.A., February 14, 1929
25. W.A., August 2, 1925